CRASH

Dick Allen and Tim Whitaker

CRASH

The Life and Times of Dick Allen

Ticknor & Fields · New York · 1989

For information about permission to reproduce selections
from this book, write to Permissions, Ticknor & Fields,
52 Vanderbilt Avenue, New York, New York 10017.

Library of Congress Cataloging-in-Publication Data
Allen, Dick.
Crash : the life and times of Dick Allen / Dick Allen and Tim Whitaker.
p.   cm.
ISBN 0-89919-657-8
1. Allen, Dick. 2. Baseball players — United States — Biography.
I. Whitaker, Tim (Tim Joseph) II. Title.
GV865.A35A3 1989   88–36820
796.357'092'4 — dc19   CIP   [B]
Printed in the United States of America
P 10 9 8 7 6 5 4 3 2 1

Thanks are gratefully given for permission to quote lyrics from the following:

"Lean on Me" by Bill Withers. Copyright © 1972, 1987 Interior Music. Used by permission of Warner/Chappell Music, Inc. All rights reserved.

"The ABC's of Love" by Morris Levy and Richard Barrett. Copyright © 1956, 1984 Longitude Music Co. All rights reserved. Reprinted by permission of Longitude Music Co.

"Sincerely" by Alan Freed and Harvey Fuqua. Copyright © 1954, 1982 Irving Music, Inc., and Arc Music Corp. Published by Liaison Two, administered by American League Music and Irving Music, Inc. All rights reserved. International copyright reserved.

"Duke of Earl" by Earl Edwards, Bernie Williams, and Eugene Dixon. Copyright © 1961 by Conrad Music, a division of Arc Music Corp. Reprinted by permission. All rights reserved.

"I'll Always Love My Mama" by Gene McFadden, Kenneth Gamble, John Whitehead, and Leon Huff. Copyright © 1973 Mighty Three Music. Administered by the Mighty Three Music Group. All rights reserved. Used by permission.

"New York, New York" by Fred Ebb and John Kander. Copyright © 1977 United Artists Corporation. All rights controlled by Unart Music Corporation. All rights of Unart Music Corporation assigned to CBS Catalogue Partnership. All rights administered by CBS Unart Catalog. International copyright secured. All rights reserved.

The picture on the first page of photographs is reproduced by kind permission of the *Arkansas Gazette*, Little Rock, Arkansas.

The picture on the top of the fifth page of photographs is reproduced by kind permission of Wide World Photos, New York, New York.

The *Sports Illustrated* cover that is reproduced on the seventh page of photographs is reproduced by kind permission of *Sports Illustrated*, New York, New York. The photographer is John Iacono.

All other pictures are reproduced by kind permission of the Bulletin/Temple Urban Archives, Philadelphia, Pennsylvania.

For Era Allen

— DA

For Hagit

— TW

To be nobody but myself — in a world which is doing its best, night and day, to make you everybody else — means to fight the hardest battle which any human being can fight, and never stop fighting.

e. e. cummings, quoted in "The Magic-Maker"

Acknowledgments

The Ballplayer and the writer would like to thank the following for their kindness and support. In no particular order they include Pete Cera, Bruce Buschel, Frank Deford, Orlando Cepeda, the Frog, Cool Papa Bell, Jack Friedman, Dorothy Daniels, Ginger, Barbara Allen, Helen Brann, Jimmy Ray Hart, Angel Cordero, Jr., Barbara Flanagan, Frances F. Freedman, Biggie, Gus, Steven Levy, Al Spitzer, Alan Halpern, Vince Rause, Joey Reynolds, Sarah Eady, Johnny Callison, Rich Ashburn, Linda Belsky Zamost, Bill White, Joe McEwen, Harvey Holiday, and Cork Smith.

And a special thanks to Jerry Romolt, who knows how to do things Dick Allen style.

Contents

Preface

We began, those of us born male in the Truman-Eisenhower years, with a bat, a ball, and a glove. "Here, son, hold the bat this way," our fathers instructed us patiently. "Keep your head down," our Little League coaches insisted, on the hard-hit ground balls. "Don't put your foot in the bucket," they all demanded when the pitch came way inside.

Our dream was to be a ballplayer. To make our dream come true, we practiced the great American pastime as it was passed on, emphasizing the fundamentals. But in secret, alone, among ourselves, we preferred to emulate the cathode showmen who flickered across our television screen. When no one was looking, we would try to basket-catch like Willie Mays or hit from both sides like Mickey Mantle or stick our head out over the plate and wiggle our bat menacingly like Frank Robinson or kick our foot to the sky to pitch like Juan Marichal. The real fun was in making our baseball cards come to life.

But in the sixties, our baseball fun ended as abruptly as a called third strike. Our determination to hang in there against the high hard one was suddenly replaced by concerns over civil rights, Vietnam, morality, peace, justice.

Try as we might, for many of us, the great American game had lost its place among the rapidly shifting priorities in our lives. We had met the enemy, and the enemy included baseball.

For the Phillies, batting third, number 15, Richie Allen.
For those of us who grew up in and around Philadelphia in the sixties, those words over the public address system at Connie Mack Stadium signaled a moment of decision: to boo or to cheer.

Our decision said a lot about who we were. It began in 1964, when Richie Allen was named Rookie of the Year as the slugging third baseman for the Philadelphia Phillies. Eight tumultuous seasons later, Dick Allen was named Most Valuable Player of the American League while playing for the Chicago White Sox. He once hit 40 home runs in a single season and in the early seventies became the highest-paid player in the major leagues.

Allen was labeled baseball's biggest outlaw. He was undisciplined and outspoken, a free spirit who abided by no rules. He was accused of missing curfews, skipping spring training, drinking on the job, getting high, fighting with teammates, having managers fired, and even doodling cryptic messages in the infield dirt. He never did want to be bothered with sportswriters. He was as enigmatic as he was recalcitrant.

Dick Allen was also the first black man in Philadelphia baseball history to win a starting job in his rookie year. The early battleground was Connie Mack Stadium, formerly Shibe Park but renamed in 1952 in honor of Cornelius McGillicuddy. For fifty seasons, from 1901 through 1950, Mack (né McGillicuddy) piloted the by and large hapless

Philadelphia Athletics. A tall, taciturn man, Mack came to embody baseball in Philadelphia through sheer longevity. Mack was an easy symbol, managing his club as he did in civvies, replete with starched white collar, dressed to the nines.

On and off the field, Mack was a disciplinarian. He forbade the use of alcohol among his players and didn't take to cursing either. But when the Jackie Robinson–led Brooklyn Dodgers came to Philadelphia to play an exhibition against the Athletics in 1947, Connie Mack made the following statement to a group of Philadelphia writers: "I'm not putting my team on the same field with that nigger."

He later relented, but for reasons known only to the scribes of Mack's day his words were never reported in the newspapers.

By the mid-sixties, Connie Mack Stadium was a tired and outdated edifice. Philadelphians moaned loud and often about the stadium's small wooden seats, the cramped aisle space, and the many steel beams that blocked their view of the playing field. They complained about the lack of adequate parking and the dangerous neighborhood.

But for me, Connie Mack Stadium was the Fantasia of ballparks. The images remain: the colorful billboards along the outfield fences — GOLDENBERG'S PEANUT CHEWS, WISE POTATO CHIPS, ALPO 100% MEAT — the huge BALLANTINE BEER scoreboard in right-center field with its bright orange three-ring logo, and the giant black-and-white LONGINES clock that sat atop that scoreboard, seemingly a million miles away.

For those of us who bore witness to Phillies baseball circa mid-to-late sixties, the real memories begin and end with

Dick Allen, perhaps the most powerful and gifted athlete in Philadelphia baseball history. Those of us who were there will never forget seeing Dick Allen hit baseballs over the FERRARO CADILLAC, COCA-COLA, and PHILCO billboards that sat high atop the left-center-field bleachers, just underneath the stadium's foreboding light towers. In the next day's newspaper there was always a picture of a parking lot attendant clutching the baseball that Allen had launched into orbit, along with an accompanying story comparing the Allen blast to those by Jimmie Foxx, one of Connie Mack's A's, or to home runs hit by Josh Gibson, the powerful black catcher who occasionally played Negro League ball in Mack's ballpark.

It may be worth noting for the sake of historical perspective that a statue of Connie Mack, resplendent in suit and tie, ever-present scorecard in hand, stands outside Philadelphia's Veterans Stadium today. In the mid-sixties, Dick Allen passed the statue every day on his way to the ballpark; at that time, the Connie Mack statue was located in a public park across the street from the stadium named in Mack's honor. When the Phillies moved to a new ballpark in 1971, so did the Mack likeness. When Allen returned to play with the Phillies in the mid-seventies near the end of his career, he passed the same statue of Mack on the way into Veterans Stadium.

When I first began contacting Dick Allen about the possibility of writing his life story, letters came back unopened and phone calls went unreturned. He seemed as resolute as ever about maintaining his privacy. Still, I persisted. Despite the controversies he created and his sometimes seemingly self-destructive behavior, I felt there was perhaps something deeply unfair about the way the people of

Philadelphia treated the young Allen in his formidable baseball years. The way I saw it, Allen's behavior in those early years was as much a reaction to the Philadelphia fans as the other way around, a strange and demented twist to the mores that normally guide the relationship between ballplayer and fan.

There was the very question of his name. Allen never felt comfortable being called Richie. Back home, in Wampum, Pennsylvania, everybody called him Dick. But when he signed with the Phillies in 1960, he was dubbed Richie Allen (and he is still so listed in *The Baseball Encyclopedia*). To this day he doesn't know how it happened or why. He speculates that he may have been named after Richie Ashburn (who, ironically, disliked being called Richie himself), the great Phillies singles hitter who helped lead the Whiz Kids to a pennant in 1950. Maybe it was a public relations idea.

Whatever the case, "Richie" sounded like a little boy's name; worse, it always sounded as if they were talking about somebody else. Finally, in the late sixties, Allen asked the Philadelphia sportswriters to please get it right.

"Don't call me Richie," he said simply. "My name is Dick."

At the time, Cassius Clay had just become Muhammad Ali, and Lew Alcindor had become Kareem Abdul-Jabbar. No Muslim considerations in Allen's case; he just wanted to be addressed by the name his mother had called him since his birth. For still inexplicable reasons, people in Philadelphia refused to honor his request. Months after Allen had made his request public, the public address announcer at Connie Mack Stadium continued to introduce Phillies number 15 as "Richie Allen."

Though nearly a decade of seasons had passed since his

glory days, the question remained: Was Dick Allen a baseball martyr or merely his own worst enemy?

Then, one spring morning, the phone rang.

"This is Dick Allen, former Phillie," said the voice.

"Dick?"

"Look, about this book, think it'll do good for anybody?"

"I do," I said.

"One thing," said Dick Allen, "I'm not telling stories about my teammates."

"Fair enough," I said.

"Another thing. I don't want to just tell my story, I want you to live it. I want you to walk in my shoes."

"All right," I said.

"Solid," said Allen. "Let's get to work."

From that moment on, Dick Allen proved good to his word, showing up for our every meeting not only on time, but often *early*.

A writer friend of mine, a former sixties rebel and a native Philadelphian, spends much of his free time these days teaching his two growing boys the fundamentals of the game.

He is a New Yorker now, a successful writer. When he talks old-time baseball with his colleagues, he tells me, they talk only of the Mick. Or DiMag. Or, worst of all, Reggie.

His two sons are inordinately curious about baseball past. They collect old baseball cards. They read *The Baseball Encyclopedia*. They are into the history.

One Saturday morning they came to him with a stack of old baseball cards. Pick your favorite, Dad, they said.

He shuffled through the cards, this friend of mine did, and threw two from the large stack on the table — Willie Mays and Dick Allen.

Which one, Dad? they asked. Who's your favorite?

My friend said he spent a long time looking at the two cards. Willie Mays they should know about.

Finally, he picked up the Dick Allen card.

Why him, Dad? they asked.

He hoped, he said, that someday he could tell them.

CRASH

•1•

The Frank Thomas Incident

On the evening of July 3, 1965, Richie Allen, the Ballplayer, threw a punch at Frank Thomas, a ballplayer on his own team.

Dick Allen recalls the punch:

> I nailed Thomas with a left hook to the jaw. He knew it was coming. I was looking for a fair one, Philadelphia-style.

After getting slugged, Thomas swung the bat he was holding, hitting Richie Allen on the left shoulder.

At the time of the altercation, Richie Allen was twenty-three, just hours from being named the starting third baseman for the National League All-Star team. The powerfully built young ballplayer was hitting a passionate .348 for the Philadelphia Phillies, having picked up where he left off the season before when he was named the National League's Rookie of the Year with 29 home runs and a .318 batting average.

Young Richie Allen's body was state-of-the-art major league: 5′11″, 180 pounds, shoulders to waist tapered in a perfect *V*, cobra-quick wrists, a blacksmith's forearms, a thoroughbred's legs — perhaps the most dramatic physique ever to have entered the game. "Stripped to the waist," a Philadelphia sportswriter wrote, "Rich Allen looks as if he could have stolen his upper torso from the Rodin Museum." Gene Mauch, the feisty thirty-nine-year-old manager of the Philadelphia team, was mesmerized by the Pennsylvania-bred phenom's hitting talents. "I wouldn't be surprised," Mauch would say to anyone who would listen, "if Richie Allen one day hits the ball to both right and left field on the same pitch. He could split the ball right in half."

In Richie Allen, Gene Mauch knew, the Phillies had found a ballplayer of Ruthian proportions. Allen's weapon was a 42-ounce bat, the heaviest bat in baseball, the biggest to be carted to the plate since Babe Ruth had done so himself. What's more, young Allen hit like the Babe, too. From the start, Richie Allen's home runs were never ordinary. They were home run caricatures, hit frighteningly hard, over billboards, over light towers, bouncing off Philadelphia row houses, sailing into the deep dark night.

On defense, at third base, Allen's role often appeared scripted by Rod Serling. He had arrived at spring training in 1964 trained as an outfielder, according to the Phillies' specifications, having spent the summer of 1963 in Triple A ball trying to master a treacherous left field in Little Rock, Arkansas.

But Gene Mauch, who felt he had a solid outfield in Covington, Gonzalez, and Callison, had another idea.

"Hey, Allen," Mauch had yelled to the young ballplayer when he was brought up to the Phillies for a cursory look at the close of the 1963 season.

"Yo," said the twenty-one-year-old outfielder.

"Ever play third base?"

"In high school, a bit," Richie Allen answered.

"Get over to third base," Mauch ordered. "You're our third baseman."

Thus Richie Allen, the Ballplayer, became the twenty-sixth player to attempt to win the third-base job for the Philadelphia Phillies franchise in six years.

From the start, his play at third base was exciting, if turbulent. He had a matador's instincts for position but lacked perspective once he came up with the ball. On ground balls, the young Allen would dive to his right à la Clete Boyer to save a two-base hit, only to get up and throw the ball five rows into the first-base seats. He could barehand a bunt in the fashion of a Brooks Robinson but would sometimes slip and fall making the throw. He made 41 errors in 1964, more than any other player in both leagues.

Not to worry, the baseball pundits said: Allen had God-given talent. He could hit with power to all fields, and for average yet; and what's more, he could run. The defense would come later. The sportswriters were lavish in their comparisons, measuring Allen favorably against baseball's very best — Mays, Mantle, Frank Robinson, Henry Aaron, all future Hall of Famers.

At the time of the altercation, Frank Thomas, Allen's teammate, was thirty-six and one of professional baseball's veteran power hitters. Over his sixteen-year career in the major leagues, Thomas would hit 286 home runs and finish with a lifetime .266 batting average. But by the summer of '65, Thomas had been relegated to the role of utilityman by Gene Mauch, the Phillies skipper. Frank Thomas was an unhappy man.

At 6'3" and 200 pounds, Thomas was lumpy and tough, like the Pittsburgh landscape of his birth. In baseball circles, Thomas was known as an agitator. For laughs he would often challenge a pitcher to throw him his hardest pitch. Then he would stand at home plate and catch it bare-handed.

Thomas and Allen were the strongest men on the Philadelphia Phillies baseball team.

Dick Allen on Frank Thomas:

> There was one thing that Frank Thomas used to do that I could never get out of my mind. He would pretend to offer his hand in a soul shake to a young player on the team, but when the player would offer his hand in return, Thomas would grab the player's thumb and bend it back hard. To Thomas, this was a big joke. But I saw too many brothers on the team with swollen thumbs to get any laughs.

Frank Thomas was a popular personality in Philadelphia. He came to the Phillies late in the '64 season from the New York Mets with a single assignment: to provide clutch power hitting for the '64 pennant-driving Phillies. Thomas had made good on that mandate, too, before fracturing his thumb on a slide into second base in the first week of that September.

While waiting for his thumb to heal, Thomas took a job as a disc jockey, cohosting a highly rated morning radio show with Uncle Phil Sheridan, a longtime Philadelphia fixture. The Uncle Phil–Frank Thomas show became a favorite of Philadelphia morning commuters. The early hours may account for the popularity of the baseball chatter the duo dished out between news, weather, and music every morning. One sample radio Thomas-ism even made the pages of *Sports Illustrated*: "Why does it take a runner longer to go from second to third than from first to second?" Answer: Because there's a short stop in between.

Dick Allen remembers how the altercation with Thomas started:

> I was down at third base fielding ground balls; Thomas was in the cage taking batting practice. Johnny Callison [another teammate] stopped by third base. He had a big grin on his face. He said, "Let's fuck with Lurch." Most of the players in the league called Thomas "the Big Donkey." But I had personal nicknames for everybody. I called Thomas "Lurch" because he reminded me of the Frankenstein character on "The Addams Family."

The summer prior to the Thomas incident, seething racial unrest had exploded onto the streets of Philadelphia, the worst of it occurring near Connie Mack Stadium, the ancient and deteriorating ballpark at 21st and Lehigh in the North Philadelphia section of the city. The "Negro riots," as they were called by one Philadelphia newspaper, had strained relations between blacks and whites in a city never known for its racial harmony. By the summer of '65, the riots had made many white people afraid to go to the ballpark.

Adding to the general surliness in and around Connie Mack Stadium that summer was the play of the home baseball team. The summer before, the Phillies had appeared the team of destiny. With twelve games to go in the season, the Phils were leading the league by six and a half games and were coming home to start a seven-game stand in Connie Mack Stadium. The World Series tickets were printed. After a fourteen-year drought, it seemed the Fall Classic would finally be coming back to Connie Mack Stadium.

What happened next was a baseball collapse of epic proportions. Some say the Phillies' dreams of a '64 pennant self-destructed when Phillies manager Gene Mauch seemed to panic during the final days of the team's skid. With ten days left in the season, Mauch abruptly scrapped his normal pitching rotation and began starting his two aces, left-hander Chris Short and right-hander Jim Bunning, with only two days' rest. Their tired arms couldn't hold up. The Phillies finished in a tie for second place, and the city went into mourning.

But by the summer of '65, the mourning period had ended. Now Philadelphians were looking for a rumble.

Dick Allen tells what happened next:

> So Callison waits until Thomas takes a big swing and a miss down at the batting cage. Then he yells, "Hey Lurch!" Thomas yells back, "You rang?" Then Callison says, "Why don't you try to bunt instead?"

Callison's gibe struck a nerve. The night before, Frank Thomas had been at the plate with runners on first and third and one out. Afraid of hitting into a double play, Thomas had tried to bunt the ball — not once, but three times, striking out awkwardly in the process. The sight of the big, burly Thomas attempting to bunt had the Philadelphia players still laughing the next morning at breakfast.

Dick Allen continues:

> But instead of answering Callison's taunts, Thomas glares down the third-base line at me and screams, "What are you trying to be, another Muhammad Clay, always running your mouth off?" Thomas knew it was Callison who had taunted him. The "Muhammad Clay" remark was meant to say a lot, and it reminded me of how he would bend back a black player's thumb for laughs.

Events, according to those who were there to witness them, escalated quickly after that.

Next thing I remember is hearing the bell ring, the signal for the regulars to come in to hit. I went down to the cage and there's Thomas, resting his elbow on a bat, waiting for me. Like I said, he knew it was coming. I went over, right in his face. I said, "Frank, I told you, that stuff don't go with me." Then I popped him, a short left to the jaw. He went down, then he got up swinging that bat. I ducked, but he caught me on the left shoulder. I just wanted to teach him a lesson. Now I wanted to kill him.

Johnny Callison, for his part, sought shelter in the Phillies dugout. "I was hiding," admits Callison. "These were big guys. I knew Richie — and I knew how this had been building. Richie was under control until Thomas took that swing at him with the bat. After that it took five guys to keep Allen off Thomas. Our shortstop, Ruben Amaro, took a shot in the chops trying to restrain Richie."

Following the fight, the Phillies still had to play baseball against the San Francisco Giants. In the seventh inning of that game, Richie Allen jolted a bases-loaded triple, a 400-foot-plus blast off the BALLANTINE BEER scoreboard in Connie Mack Stadium. It was his third hit of the night.

One inning later, Frank Thomas came to the plate as a pinch hitter and homered.

Dick Allen recalls what happened after the game:

My shoulder was swollen to twice its size and hurt like hell from where Thomas had hit me with the bat. But as far as I was concerned, the fight was over. After Thomas hit that pinch-hit home run, I walked up and shook his hand. In our own way, the way two ballplayers do, we were getting over it. We were back to the business at hand, trying to win ballgames.

Fights like the Allen-Thomas altercation are common in baseball, usually quickly forgotten, smoothed over by front

office types with hurried handshakes between the partici-
pants and mumbled apologies. But in 1965, the Philadelphia
Phillies front office was still reeling from the club's collective nervous breakdown of 1964. It was a front office
determined to show disgruntled fans that it could act
decisively.

Dick Allen recalls what happened after the game:

> Gene Mauch called me into his office and told me they had
> just released Thomas. He didn't have to — the news had
> already made it to the clubhouse. He said he was tired of
> putting up with the way Thomas picked on other players.
> He then stuck his head out of his office and yelled to
> everyone in the clubhouse, "If I hear one word about any of
> this to the press, it's going to cost the guilty party fifteen
> hundred bucks." Then he turned to me and said, "And if I
> hear anything from you, Allen, twenty-five hundred!"

Angered by his release, Thomas turned to television and
radio, where he had a lot of friends from his Uncle Phil days.
His assessment of Richie Allen, though neither eloquent nor
original, was a direct hit. "Certain guys can dish it out," the
newly exiled Thomas cried, "but can't take it."

When reporters asked Richie Allen for his side of the
story, the Ballplayer shrugged his shoulders.

"What fight?" he deadpanned.

Having been told it was in his best interest to stay quiet,
Allen refused to comment — even at home. "Know how *I*
found out about the fight with Frank Thomas?" recalls
Barbara Moore, Allen's wife at the time. "I opened the
paper and read it the next morning. I remember I woke
Dick up and said, 'Hey, what's all this?' He just opened one
eye, and said, 'Don't worry, all that'll blow over.' I knew
better. Things that happened to Dick *never* blew over."

Dick Allen on Gene Mauch's decision to release Thomas:

> I begged Gene to release me instead of Thomas. But Mauch said, "What? Are you kidding? We get a hitter like you once in a lifetime!" I asked Mauch why we couldn't tell the truth, but he just looked at me like I was crazy.

Word of Thomas's release became big news in Philadelphia and in baseball circles around the country. In the days that followed, Thomas continued to complain that he had been wronged. "I've always liked Richie," Thomas lamented to writers. "I've tried to help him."

To this day, Johnny Callison thinks there are a lot of baseball people who still don't know the real reason the Phillies released Thomas. "Thomas rubbed a *lot* of people the wrong way," says the former Phillies outfielder and Allen teammate. "Mauch wanted him gone — and here was his excuse. People just assumed Allen was the guy that got Thomas fired. But Thomas got himself fired when he swung that bat at Richie. In baseball, you don't swing a bat at another player — ever."

Rich Ashburn, today a Phillies broadcaster, was a former roommate of Frank Thomas. "Frank wasn't the most enlightened guy in baseball," recalls the former Whiz Kid. "He didn't get the tag 'Big Donkey' for his smarts. A lot of guys in baseball could give the needle, but Thomas never knew when to quit. He wasn't an evil guy. His timing was just always off. When he gave the needle to Rich, he bit off more than he bargained for."

There are those in baseball, former first baseman and onetime Allen roomie Bill White among them, who feel the Thomas fight and its subsequent cover-up by the Philadelphia Phillies front office forever diminished the career of one of baseball's most promising young stars. "Baseball should never forget the Allen-Thomas fiasco," White says. "There's an important lesson here. When Dick Allen came to the big leagues, he was a kid in love with the game. Baseball was all that mattered. After the Thomas incident, the love was taken right out of him. There's historical significance in how that was handled."

Dick Allen on the Thomas aftermath:

I knew releasing Thomas was going to be big trouble. Mother had always taught me to tell the truth, and now the Phillies were telling me not to. I went to my locker, sat down, and fought back the tears. I loved baseball, but not like this. I just wanted to play the game. After the Thomas fight, all I wanted to do was go home. to Wampum, where the game had been fun.

•2•

Little Rock, Arkansas

Then again, there are those students of the Dick Allen saga who believe that things first began to go awry for the powerful slugger in Little Rock, Arkansas, in the summer of 1963.

Trouble came on the very first pitch of the '63 season. The Ballplayer has vivid recall:

> The ball was hit out to me in left field. A lazy fly ball. I froze, then I took a few steps in, and the ball flew over my head. I missed the ball because I was scared. I don't mind saying it.

Allen had signed with the Philadelphia Phillies in 1960 right out of Wampum High School. He had spent his first full season of baseball in Magic Valley, Utah, and in 1962 had played Double A ball in Williamsport, Pennsylvania, where he had lost the batting title in the final game of the season to Jimmy Ray Hart, the future Giants third baseman.

The 1963 season was the first for Triple A baseball in Little Rock, an auspicious event in itself. To mark the occasion, Governor Orval Faubus — the same Governor

Faubus who had garnered national notoriety for attempting to block black teenagers from attending Little Rock's Central High School in 1957 — was on hand to throw out the first ball. "I knew who he was," says Allen of the former Arkansas governor, "and I sure as hell knew what he was famous for, but I didn't know what he was doing there."

That opening night, Little Rock's Ray Winder Stadium was filled to its 7,000-seat capacity. When Dick Allen took his position in the outfield as the starting left fielder for the Arkansas Travelers, he became the first black ballplayer to play professional baseball in the state of Arkansas.

"When I arrived at the park," says Allen, "there were people marching around outside with signs. One said, DON'T NEGRO-IZE BASEBALL. Another, NIGGER GO HOME. They were the same signs that greeted me the day I landed at the Little Rock airport. Here, in my mind, I thought Jackie Robinson had Negro-ized baseball sixteen years earlier."

The Allen protests were organized by Amos Guthridge, a diehard Arkansas segregationist. During the Freedom Rider days of the early sixties Guthridge had attempted to organize a southern fried freedom ride to Hyannisport to visit the Kennedys. "The man was an embarrassment," says Jim Bailey, a sportswriter who covered Allen's Little Rock debut in 1963 for the *Arkansas Gazette*. "When I saw Guthridge and his boys marching around the ballpark, I felt like hiding under a rock."

Out in left field, during the playing of the National Anthem, the Ballplayer recalls repeating Psalm 23, the words from the Bible that his mother taught him as a child:

Yea though I walk through the valley of the shadow of
    death,

I will fear no evil:
for thou art with me . . .

Then, first pitch, the botched fly ball. "When Richie misjudged that ball in left field," says Bailey, today still a sportswriter for the *Gazette,* "it sounded like somebody had swatted a gigantic beehive with a baseball bat."

Later in the game, at the plate, the Ballplayer made up for his opening miscue by belting two doubles. "The second one, I crushed," recalls Allen. "*Blam!* I remember wanting those Little Rock folks to feel my strength. My inner strength." His second double set up the Travelers' winning rally. "After that, I could feel the fans relax a bit. I even began to think that maybe, *maybe,* I could fit in down here."

The manager of the Arkansas Travelers was Frank Lucchesi. Lucchesi, thirty-seven, had managed the Ballplayer in Williamsport the previous season. Following Allen's opening night performance, Lucchesi was ecstatic. "He kept clapping me on the back and telling me things were going to be all right," remembers Allen. "I liked Frank. His style was to tell me to pick a stick out of the bat rack and go up there and have fun. In that way, he had my number. But that night he didn't understand me at all. He was thinking about the doubles. I was thinking about my life."

Allen remembers showering slowly and leaving the clubhouse late the night of that season opener in Little Rock.

I wanted to be alone. I needed to sort it all out. I waited until the clubhouse cleared out before walking to the parking lot. When I got to my car, I found a note on the windshield. It said, DON'T COME BACK AGAIN NIGGER. I felt scared

and alone, and, what's worse, my car was the last one in the
parking lot. There might be something more terrifying than
being black and holding a note that says NIGGER in an empty
parking lot in Little Rock, Arkansas, in 1963. But if there is,
it hasn't crossed my path yet.

Only one thing mattered to Dick Allen that summer of
'63 — making the Phillies club. "I was hungry to play in the
bigs," he explains. "I'd hit nine home runs with the Phillies
in spring training, the most on the club, serious shots
among them."

But in 1963, the Phillies lineup included Wes Covington,
Don Demeter, and Johnny Callison, three good outfielders.
"Still," wonders the Ballplayer all these years later, "I
thought they could have used that big bat of mine *somewhere*."

Allen has two theories why the Phillies didn't bring him
up that spring of '63. "Reason one," he says, "I'd told
[Phillies general manager] John Quinn prior to the season
that I wanted a fifty-dollar raise. I'd hit .329 for Williamsport in the Eastern League in 1962. The team finished
with a fourteen-game lead. Where I come from, western
Pennsylvania steel country, a man makes sure he gets a
raise for work well done. All I wanted was fifty bucks. I
needed to feel I was making progress. But this was not the
way Quinn saw things. He said if I held out for a raise, I
would spend another season in the minors. I did, and Little
Rock was the result."

In addition, Allen believes that the Phillies had a hidden
agenda: to break the race barrier in Arkansas. "Sixty-three
was the first season for Triple A ball down there and the
first season with the Phillies as parent club — and no
blacks," explains Allen. "They had no choice but to bust it.

I didn't know anything about the race issue in Arkansas and didn't care. Maybe if the Phillies had called me in, man to man, like the Dodgers had done with Jackie, and said, 'Dick, this is what we have in mind, it's going to be very difficult, but we're with you' — at least then I would have been better prepared. I'm not saying I would have liked it. But I *would* have known what to expect."

Before reporting to Little Rock that spring, Allen married Barbara Moore, a girl he had courted while playing Double A ball in Williamsport the season before. He had planned to bring his new wife with him to Little Rock. But Era Allen, the Ballplayer's strong-willed mother, thought the idea ill advised: "My mother got very concerned. What black mother wouldn't? We had all seen the pictures of army troops walking beside black teenagers up the steps of Little Rock's Central High in 1957. The way I saw it, all those kids wanted to do was go to school — all this kid Dickie Allen wanted to do was play ball. Mother told me it would probably be a better idea to keep Barbara at home until things settled down."

Upon reporting to Little Rock, Allen was given housing with a family on the black side of town. "I didn't live near the other ballplayers, and I didn't dare visit them — and I guess the white players didn't feel comfortable visiting me," he recalls. "I got lonely fast." Right from the start, Allen says he was taught a lesson he would never forget: "There were two sets of rules in Little Rock, one for the Arkansas Travelers and one for Dick Allen, the black left fielder for the Arkansas Travelers. That didn't go with me. From that day on, I decided if there was ever a double standard again, I would be the beneficiary, and not the other way around."

*   *   *

Dick Allen batted .290 for the Arkansas Travelers and hit 33 home runs in the summer of '63. Seventeen of those home runs he hit in Little Rock's home ballpark, and 15 of them were hit to right field. "Pitchers would throw Rich the slow, breaking, away stuff, and he would stay right with it and jerk it to right," says *Gazette* sportswriter Bailey. "Allen had tremendous bat control and the patience to stay with a pitch, the best I've ever seen."

That summer, the Ballplayer soon made believers of the Little Rock baseball faithful. Proof came in a late-season poll of Arkansas Travelers fans when Allen was voted the team's Most Popular Player. But off the field, Allen was often treated like a second-class citizen — and worse. "One night I went to get a cold can of soda from a machine a block away from my rooming house," he recalls. "I was jogging home with the can in my hand. It was a rare off-day and a typically hot Arkansas night. But it had just begun to cool off a bit and I needed to loosen up. Next thing, a squad car comes by and the police put me up against a wall. Then they spread-eagle me against their car. One of the two policemen pulls his gun. They ask me if I stole the can of soda. When I tell them no, they ask me why I was running. I tell them that this is America, and it is my understanding that running is legal in America. The two policemen don't say a word. It was like they had never looked at it that way before. They just let me go. But for weeks afterward I had this vision of catching a bullet in the back just for being thirsty."

All season, Allen continued to receive threatening notes. "They were left on my car, taped to the clubhouse door, and sent in the mail," he says. The Ballplayer remembers one note in particular left on the windshield of his car during an early-season road trip: "The note said, 'Allen — take the field again and you're a dead man.' I didn't tell Lucchesi. Every other time he had tried to convince me it was an isolated incident. I wasn't going to give him the chance to tell me that again. Frank looked at Arkansas in a different way. He married a girl from Pine Bluff, Arkansas. He saw the bright side. I was looking to save my ass. I was *living* my side."

Shortly after that particular death threat, the Ballplayer began hearing gunshots late at night outside the house where he was staying. "I would just start to fall asleep, and — bang, bang, bang — rapid-fire shots. Were they meant for me? Or just meant to upset our little black neighborhood? I wasn't sure. But either way, it wasn't a good sign."

Allen decided he had seen and heard enough. He telephoned Coy Allen, his oldest brother, and told him he was coming home. Then Allen called John Quinn, the Phillies general manager, and gave him the same message. Forty-eight hours later, Coy Allen, John Quinn, and John Ogden, the scout who had signed Allen, flew down to Little Rock to assess the situation for themselves.

"Up to that point, the Phillies had no interest in how Dick was making out down there," claims Coy Allen today. "They were either totally unaware of the situation or they just didn't care. They did care about Dickie's home run production and batting average, but not how he was making out in an all-white Deep South environment. When he told them he was thinking about going home to Wampum, *then* they cared. Were the gunshots in the neighborhood meant for Dick? I don't know. The police confirmed there had been reports of gunshots. But there was no follow-up. I will say this, it was rough down there. I wasn't sure I could get through to Dick. He was determined to come home. Then I said the right thing. I told him if he returned to Wampum, he'd have to get a job — and in Wampum, I reminded him, there are only two places for a man to work: the steel mill or the cement mill. After he heard that, he seemed more willing to stick it out."

Shortly after Coy's visit, Barbara Allen, the Ballplayer's new bride, joined her husband in Little Rock.

"Dick and I didn't do much down there except stay home," recalls Barbara Moore. "My home state was Pennsylvania, same as Dick's. Arkansas seemed very far away. I had to learn how to act. For instance, I learned to always make sure to go to the bathroom *before* going to see Dick play at the ballpark. I would never go to the refreshment stand. It was best to stay in my seat, out in the open. I heard the word 'nigger' a lot that summer in Little Rock. It was never someone coming up and saying it right in my face. It was more like the word was around me all the time. Know when I would hear it? When Dick came up to bat. That was when I could count on hearing it."

In researching Dick Allen's 1963 season in Little Rock, I inadvertently stumbled on a memo sent to *Sports Illustrated* in April 1964. The author of the memo was one Orville Henry, a sportswriter for the *Arkansas Gazette*. The memo — not written for publication — reported on Allen's Triple A season for the Arkansas Travelers and repudiated almost everything Allen later told me about what happened to him in Little Rock.

Such "backgrounders" are common at the Time/Life

sports weekly. With Allen off to a hot start in the spring of '64, *Sports Illustrated* was merely accumulating historical data for the many feature stories that the Allen bat would surely bring in the months and years ahead.

But what was different about this particular backgrounder was the highly personal, largely nonbaseball nature of Henry's findings. The seven-page memo asserted that things hadn't been so bad for Allen in Little Rock after all, that in fact Allen lived in a "lonely little world full of fear."

In addition, the report also asserted:

- That Allen ranked as one of the all-time favorites at Little Rock and was treated in kind.
- That Allen gave misleading answers to reporters' questions — including the assertion that he was single.
- That he had made no effort to meet people in the black community and that he wasn't close to any of his fellow Traveler teammates.
- That his unhappiness in Little Rock stemmed from shyness and the difficult travel and playing conditions.
- That Travelers manager Frank Lucchesi found Allen sensitive and self-centered.

The report included a quote from Lucchesi: "[Allen] is not concerned about what town we're in, or what park, or what team we're playing. He's interested in Richie, and hitting. He's not thinking about his fielding, or throwing, or team play. To tell the truth, he's had no abuse at all."

I decided to ask the Ballplayer pointedly about Henry's conclusions.

The Writer: This report says you comprehended little except your own fear.

Allen: That's cracker talk. I was the first black ballplayer in Little Rock, Arkansas. That's not a scary situation? Let me meet the man who wrote this. I think *he* needs a short lesson in the meaning of fear.

The Writer: He also says that you were treated well by fans.

Allen: There were fans in Little Rock who truly loved the game, and for some of them color didn't matter. I gathered my strength from them. But there were others who got off on racial intimidation. Between innings, coming in from the outfield to the dugout, I would hear the voices — "Hey, Chocolate Drop" or "Watch your back, nigger." I would look up, but I could never find the guy who made the remarks. Racist fans have a way of hissing and mumbling under their breath that makes them hard to locate. Black players know this and after a while learn not to look up. I would have loved to go a round with any one of them. I think a one-on-one slugfest with one of those racist cowards would have given me all the release I needed.

The Writer: It also says you gave reporters misleading answers.

Allen: True. I never understood what the sportswriters wanted from me down there. They would sit me down for these long interviews about my family and home life in Wampum. But the next day there would never be anything except a story about that night's game in the paper. It seemed they wanted to find out about me so they could justify some feelings they had about black people.

The Writer: The report says you weren't close to anybody in the "Negro community" or any of your teammates, for that matter.

Allen: How would he know? No writer ever visited my side of town. No one ever came to my door. He never met the people in my neighborhood. As for my teammates, I was friendly but cautious. A friend of mine, a black Vietnam vet, once told me that he never turned his back on white guys from the South in combat. I felt that way in Little Rock. I knew there were teammates of mine who hated my black ass. You can feel that kind of thing. Rather than have guys treat me one way to my face and another behind my back, I just kept my distance.

The Writer: He quotes Lucchesi as saying you were self-centered and suffered no abuse at all.

Allen: What would Lucchesi know about abuse? While I was laying in bed listening to gunshots, he was eating at the best restaurants in Little Rock. As for being self-centered, Lucchesi had only one thing in mind that year: managing in the major leagues. Dick Allen had only one thing in mind: playing in the major leagues. Lucchesi may not have liked the fact that I was going to get there before him.

The Writer: Why would this reporter turn in such a negative report?

Allen: Beats me. Why don't you go down there and find out?

Little Rock, Arkansas, June 1987. First stop, Ray Winder Field, home of the Arkansas Travelers. A minor league classic: tidy, freshly painted, colorful. Old-fashioned billboards line the outfield fences: STINGER SAM AUTO PARTS,

K-MART, COLEMAN MILK & ICE CREAM, and (yes) AUNT JEMIMA CORNMEAL & CORN BREAD. Real grass, neatly manicured.

Early afternoon, and some of the Traveler team members are casually taking infield practice, others are shagging fly balls lazily in the outfield. Seven black faces on the field, including a fancy-fielding first baseman wearing number 15. On the way into town from the airport, a black cab driver, unsolicited, tells me proudly that the mayor of Little Rock is a black woman.

Sitting next to me in the ballpark is Jim Bailey, the *Arkansas Gazette* sportswriter who was assigned to cover the Travelers' '63 season with Orville Henry, the sportswriter who wrote the Allen backgrounder for *Sports Illustrated*.

Before getting to other things, Bailey wants to tell me about the dump. "The dump" is what Arkansas baseball fans called the left-field area in Ray Winder Stadium in 1963. "I wish you could have seen it," says Bailey, pointing to left field. "That whole area was gouged with holes, and there was a hill that ran straight up to the fence. I saw outfielders fall flat on their face many times on routine fly balls."

Bailey tells me it was considered a cruel twist of fate for any Arkansas Traveler unlucky enough to draw the left-field assignment. "Rich wasn't the best outfielder to come through Arkansas," Bailey explains, "but he wasn't the worst either. Fact is, by the end of the '63 season he was handling it as well as anybody." And, in fact, Bailey notes, the Ballplayer was the last Arkansas player to have to handle the left-field dump. The Phillies hired landscapers to come down to even out the whole area before the start of the '64 season.

I ask Bailey about the *Gazette*'s coverage of Allen's '63 season. Was race an issue? "We were told by our editors not to refer to the fact that Allen was the first black to play here," he says. "The paper had won two Pulitzer Prizes for editorial writing during the Central High crisis in '57. We had taken a tough stand — discrimination was wrong, period. But the paper was still reeling from the fallout of all that. There were sensitivities. The editors decided we'd be better off not getting things all stirred up again."

Orville Henry, the sportswriter contracted by *Sports Illustrated* in 1964 to file the report on Allen's '63 season, is still writing for the *Arkansas Gazette*, though these days he is best known for his coverage of the Arkansas Razorbacks football team.

While waiting to interview Henry at the paper's offices, I look through back issues of the *Arkansas Gazette* on microfilm. The coverage of Allen in that '63 season proves Bailey's memory correct: The reporting was precise and limited to game action. No mention of race — save one curious description of Allen from an April 21, 1963, Orville Henry column:

> In manner and speech Allen shows good background and a measure of sophistication. He's one of eight children of a onetime truck driver who owns seven trucks now used in long-distance hauling out of the Pittsburgh area.
> He performs, though, with the typical loose all-out exuberance of his race.

Twenty-three years have passed since Orville Henry sent *Sports Illustrated* his report on Allen's '63 season. After we shake hands, I tell him that I have a copy of the report and ask if he'd like to review it before our conversation. He tells me not to take it out of my briefcase. He does agree to let me ask questions.

The Writer: What kind of kid was Richie Allen?

Henry: A frightened kid, and unduly so. Maybe in his shoes things looked different. But he lied and invented things to help his self-esteem. He created a world in which he could look better. You get that with black athletes sometimes.

The Writer: You said in your report that Allen lived in "a lonely little world, full of fear."

Henry: Like a lot of black people back then, I'm sure Richie had heard a lot about the 1957 Central High crisis. I'm sure it had him worried. Yet if you look it up, you'll see that the Central High situation proved to be one of the most peaceful in the whole civil rights movement. Besides, Richie Allen never experienced the *real* Little Rock.

The Writer: Would he have been welcome in the real Little Rock?

Henry: In 1963? If he had been my guest, he could have dined in any Little Rock restaurant. But he never asked.

Before leaving the *Arkansas Gazette,* I ask around the newsroom for directions to 1121 Cross Street, the address where Allen stayed in 1963 while playing for the Travelers. No one in the paper's editorial offices seems to know where it is — except for a heavyset black sportswriter named Wadie Moore, Jr. Moore tells me he lives in a neighborhood adjacent to Allen's old neighborhood. His deadline past, he volunteers to show me around.

When we get in the car, Moore tells me he remembers Allen's season in Little Rock well. "I was only thirteen years old in 1963," he says, "but I remember him like yesterday. When Allen came here to play ball, it was an exciting day for black people. Allen didn't just integrate baseball in Little Rock, he integrated life. Before he got here, black folks who went to the ballpark sat together in a separate section in right field. His being here opened all that up. After him, we could sit anywhere we wanted, and believe me we did just that."

Negotiating his way through the streets of Little Rock, Moore tells me how as a kid he used to hang around the Little Rock ballpark hoping to get a few words with Allen. "He didn't say much," Moore recalls, "but when he did, there was something about the way he talked that made you want to listen. He used to talk baseball to me. He'd give little pointers. Explain the game to me. It meant a lot to me hearing this from the only professional black baseball player in the state."

Moore pulls the car in front of a small single-frame house with white aluminum siding: 1121 Cross Street.

We go up to the door, but when we ring the bell there's no answer. Moore, taking the initiative, decides to conduct a house-to-house survey along Cross Street. But twenty-four years later, nobody remembers Allen. As we're about to get into our car, Moore spots an older black man leaning against a fence. He asks the man if he remembers Richie Allen.

"The Allen who played in the big leagues?" the man asks.

"Yes sir," says Moore.

"You know, I do remember him living there," he says, pointing to 1121. "Used to admire the way that boy was built. Don't remember much else, though. Seemed to mind his own business."

Moore asks the man if there's anyone else in the neighborhood who might remember.

"Would have to say no," the man says. "People he stayed with there at 1121, they're dead and gone. All the neighbors are different. Why you ask?"

Moore points to me. "This man's doing a book on him," he says.

"Got yourself a subject there, son," the man says. "First black ballplayer to play in Little Rock. You know that?"

Back in the car, I tell Moore about the conflicting evidence regarding Allen's 1963 season. I tell him of Allen's memories — the harassment, the threatening notes, the gunshots; I tell him about Orville Henry's report and about the Frank Lucchesi quote.

Then, driving me back to my hotel room, Wadie Moore, Jr., begins to tell me the truth as he sees it.

"I know what Dick Allen was up against in 1963, but I was too young to be of much help," he begins. "Certain things you learn when you're black and you grow up down here. Basic things, but if you don't know them you're in trouble. One, if a car comes up from behind, always turn around and look right into the car. That way the people in the car know you've seen their faces. You can identify them. It also puts you in a position to duck anything that's thrown at you. Back in Dick Allen's day, I used to dodge empty pop bottles all the time walking home from the ballpark after a Travelers game.

"The police gave black folks no peace back then. I got stopped one night three times going to my girlfriend's house. They didn't just ask you for your driver's license, it was spread-eagle, against the car, gun to the back of the neck. By the third time I was stopped that night, I thought I was history. They were looking for somebody who was black. I was black. Understand, I'm not saying there aren't good people in Little Rock, then or now. But this is a tough town for black people. That's a fact. Now see, the difference is, I grew up down here. I knew how to get by. But imagine a black kid coming down to all this in 1963 from a little integrated town in Pennsylvania. Guy like that doesn't stand a chance."

•3•

No Place Like Home

The Ballplayer is driving the Pennsylvania Turnpike with
the writer, having left Philadelphia on this bright April
morning, the start of another baseball season, for a seven-
hour ride west in Big Blue, the Ballplayer's '74 Lincoln
Continental.

Our destination on this day: Wampum, Pennsylvania,
home for the Ballplayer.

Big Blue is Allen's fondest possession. The Ballplayer
bought the car in his last season with the Chicago White
Sox for $10,000 and says the car is worth at least that much
today. Allen keeps the car in immaculate condition and
loves to talk of his many travels across the country at the
helm of the wide-bodied, baby blue Lincoln. He has more
than two hundred thousand miles on the car but talks of
keeping it in shape for his children's children.

So compulsively fastidious is Allen about Big Blue that
on long drives he often exits a road at random and
searches for a car wash. He also speaks of Big Blue in the
third person. "The big fellow's been looking forward to
this ride," he says at the start of our trip. "Haven't you,
boy?"

Behind the wheel, Allen looks young enough to still be playing ball. His cheeks have retained the slightly rounded, vaguely adolescent shape of his early playing days, giving him a boyish look that softens his otherwise rugged appearance. His mustache and goatee are neatly trimmed, as are his sideburns, and he wears dark heavy eyeglass frames, not unlike the Buddy Holly–style glasses he sported in his early Philadelphia years. He is wearing lizard-skin boots and a cowboy hat, trademarks both.

Allen hasn't played major league baseball in more than a decade. He finished his fifteen-year career in 1977 with a brief and unpleasant stint with Charlie Finley's Oakland A's, having also played with the Philadelphia Phillies, the St. Louis Cardinals, the Los Angeles Dodgers, and the Chicago White Sox.

Yet today, in his mid-forties, Allen remains a remarkable physical specimen. With a 34-inch waist, he has the arms and upper body of a middleweight contender and if called upon could still fit into his Phillies rookie uniform. His wrists remain quick enough to lash a golf ball effortlessly, as he does when the spirit moves him, some 400 yards against the net of a driving range near one of his current residences in Hollywood.

On the turnpike, the Ballplayer pushes Big Blue a little past the speed limit, not enough to draw attention but always making good time. He is a knowledgeable road warrior. On the road, Dick Allen likes to say, one can find ultimate peace. For Allen, the automobile is a meditative chamber on wheels. Sometimes, as in those tumultuous times when he was deciding whether to quit big league baseball smack in the glory days of his career, the road gave him the solitude to reconsider; other times, when marital and professional responsibilities pressed uncomfortably close, the road became a place to hide.

"Back in the bad days of Philadelphia," Allen confides to me, resting his hands against the steering wheel of Big Blue, "soon as we got a day off, I would pack the kids in the car, grab the wife, and head for Wampum. There, I knew I'd just be Dick Allen. It was the one place I could go where I knew the boos and all that tension down at the yard couldn't follow. I was outside their orbit."

Today, Allen's trips home to Wampum are solitary ones. His marriage to Barbara Moore ended in 1981, following a fire that destroyed their rambling farmhouse in Pennsylvania's lush Bucks County. His three children — Teri, Dick Jr., and Button, all college-educated, have remained close to their mother. The Ballplayer's relationship with his ex-wife and his three children has remained tumultuous in the years following the divorce.

Allen exits the turnpike after a few hours of driving, stopping at a food and gas joint, a truckers' haven in Pennsylvania Dutch country familiar to the Ballplayer from his many Philadelphia–Wampum turnpike expeditions. Waiting for the food to arrive, the writer scans the box scores in the morning sports section. The Ballplayer shows little interest. "When I'm home in Los Angeles people say to me, 'Hey Rich, how 'bout those Dodgers?' " He laughs. "I always say, 'Yeah, how 'bout 'em!' But I have no idea. I sometimes pick up a broomstick and play stickball with the kids in the neighborhood. I care who wins then. But the Dodgers? The Phillies? Why should I care? I love the game. But I've never been a fan."

When the food arrives, Allen bows his head in prayer, as he does before every meal, no matter the circumstance, this time thanking God for his own good health and the health of his companion.

Over lunch, the Ballplayer does show interest in a story in the same newspaper on Bo Jackson, the young American League slugger for the Kansas City Royals. "This man I worry for," he says after reading of a poor early-season Jackson performance against the Yankees. "He's got power, which means he'll hit a lot of home runs. But he'll also strike out a lot. He knows he can play more than one sport well — that gives him confidence. It also makes him bigger than life. That makes for a lot of built-in drama. That makes for an easy mark."

After lunch, back on the road again, the Ballplayer fires up a Kent Golden Light, his current brand. When Dick Allen is relaxed, stories and anecdotes tumble out in random bursts, punctuated by warm, generous laughs; in good moods, his conversation roams free, until he finds a sweet spot; there he'll spend time, expanding, alluding, espousing, waxing metaphoric. Close friends of Dick Allen know to wait for such soliloquies.

At the moment, the Ballplayer is relaxed.

On Roberto Clemente: "There was a cat who could gig. He played the right-field wall in Forbes Field like Oscar Peterson working the piano. As a kid, I made a study of Roberto. I noticed when a hitter took a wide turn around first base, he would sometimes gun the ball back to first behind the runner instead of throwing it into second. He used to catch a lot of guys that way. Now it's years later and I'm up against the Pirates. I hit the ball to right field, Clemente country. I round the bag real wide, but instead of stopping I stutter-step and keep on running. When Clemente throws the ball to first to try to catch me, I'm already on second base, standing up."

On the possibility of being traded to the San Francisco Giants in the sixties: "I used to beg Giants manager Herman Franks to trade for me. At the time the Giants were thinking of trading Jimmy Ray Hart for me. I thought it was going to happen. What a Giants lineup that would have been — McCovey, Cepeda, Bonds, Willie Mays, a kid named Dick Allen, Marichal on the mound, dig? Think the brothers could have inflicted a little damage?"

On Mickey Mantle: "We're playing the Yankees in spring training, '65. Mantle's on first, I'm playing third. One of the Yankees hits a rope to right center. Now here comes Mantle, he's heading for third, right for me. I can see it's going to be close. There's a huge swirl of dust. The umpire's right in there with us. When the dust finally settles, the ump looks down at both of us sprawled on the ground and shakes his head. 'I've never smelled so much booze in my life,' he tells me and Mantle. 'Get off your asses before you set each other on fire.' "

In more pensive moods, Dick Allen's words come out softer and with more emotion, but with the same mastery of language.

It is one of the many ironies of Allen's career in baseball that he never used his sophisticated communicative skills to dispel trouble during his playing days. Instead, occasional audiences with sympathetic writers notwithstanding, he withdrew from the working press, refusing in most cases to go on the record with his side of the story in the many controversies that plagued his career. "All I wanted to do was play baseball" is the way he explains it. "Those guys with the notebooks were trying to take my mind off my job. That made them the natural enemy."

Two hours outside of Wampum, Allen's conversation takes a sudden serious turn.

Dick Allen is talking about his baseball career.

"I wonder how good I could have been," he begins softly. "It could have been a joy, a celebration. Instead, I played angry. In baseball, if a couple of things go wrong for you, and those things get misperceived, or distorted, you get a label. After a while, the label becomes you, and you become the label, whether that's really you or not. I was labeled an outlaw, and after a while that's what I became."

In his fifteen seasons of major league baseball, Allen hit 351 home runs, and he batted .300 or better seven times. He led the American League in homers and slugging percentage in 1972 and 1974, snagged Rookie of the Year honors in 1964, and was named Most Valuable Player in the American League while playing for the Chicago White Sox in 1972. He made the All-Star team six times. He finished with a lifetime batting average of .292. A remarkable career, by any standard.

Yet in the ten seasons since his last major league baseball game, Allen has been asking himself that same question over and over again.

I wonder how good I could have been.

Now, having said it out loud, he can think of nothing more to say.

Finally, near sunset, the Ballplayer guides Big Blue off the Pennsylvania Turnpike, exit 8, Beaver Falls. Buoyed by the familiar surroundings, he sucks in the cool Pennsylvania country air and surveys the great expanse of green all around him.

"Home," he sighs, reaching for a Kent Golden Light on the dashboard. "Here, little changes."

*   *   *

Dick Allen pilots Big Blue through Wampum slowly, pointing out the cement plant, the town's new golf course, and,
up on a hill, off the main road, Era Allen's house, a comfortable six-bedroom rancher that Allen bought for his
mother in 1960 after signing his first major league contract.
  Located thirty miles northwest of Pittsburgh, Wampum
was once an Indian trading post. Today, it's reminiscent of
Andy Griffith's Mayberry, with its small Mom-and-Pop
shops and 1,045 God-fearing citizens of melting-pot descent.
Once a hard-working steel- and cement-producing town,
Wampum has fallen on hard times in recent years. Layoffs
and plant closings have sent unemployment sky high, and
all along the town's main street men with nothing much to
do linger in small groups killing an afternoon. Much of the
small town's economic anguish, however, is discreetly
camouflaged by the scenic mountainous countryside of western Pennsylvania.

  Back when Dick Allen was playing major league baseball,
newspaper headline writers would often make puns about
the unlikely name of his hometown — calling the Ballplayer "the Wampum Warrior" or, after a big home run, writing "Allen Wamps One." *The Sporting News*, the baseball
journal of record, once published a big map of Pennsylvania
with an arrow pointing to his hometown under the headline
PHILLIES ROOKIE PUTS WAMPUM ON THE MAP.

  The Ballplayer drives through Wampum's sole major
intersection and stops the car in front of a small four-story
building with a squared-off institutional look.

  "This was Wampum High," he says, pointing proudly to
the building. "Now defunct."

  Dick Allen graduated "somewhere in the back third" of
the 1960 Wampum High class of 146 students. "I was too

interested in ball to be much of a student," he says without apology. "I remember one day when a teacher made us all stand up and tell the class what we wanted to be when we grew up. Kids were saying they wanted to be mechanics, nurses, teachers. I stood up and said I was going to be a ballplayer. The whole class laughed. People in Wampum didn't set goals like that for themselves. But I knew baseball was my future life."

Ironically, Wampum, Pennsylvania, is better known for basketball than baseball, thanks in large part to the Allen family. All five of the Allen boys — Coy, Caesar, Hank, Dickie, and Ron — were All-State in basketball at Wampum High. In 1958, Allen brothers Hank, Ronnie, and Dick — future major league baseball players all three — played hoops together for the Wampum five. Both younger brother Ronnie and older brother Hank would later attend college on basketball scholarships. If not for baseball, Dick — like Hank and Ron — would have played college basketball too. "I would have liked to play college hoops," says the Ballplayer. "I had schools interested. But it was never a consideration. The family had their mind on getting Mother a new house. We knew that my ability to hit the long ball would get us it."

By his senior year Allen was captain and a starting guard on the Wampum High basketball team, a team that rolled over opponents handily on its way to a class B championship. His coach was L. Butler Hennon, a legend in western Pennsylvania basketball circles. Hennon regularly fashioned championship basketball teams, usually with fewer than fifty boys to choose from, the smallest number in the state. Coach Hennon used old-school tactics to get results. Visitors to practice sessions in Wampum High's bandbox gym would often be startled to see Hennon's teams suited up in rubber galoshes and eyeglasses partially covered with black tape. The galoshes, Coach Hennon would explain to onlookers, made his players feel light on their feet come game time. The taped glasses kept his players from looking down at the ball while dribbling.

The Ballplayer is explaining this and the history of Wampum basketball to me from behind the wheel of Big Blue when suddenly a voice calls from the sidewalk.

"Hey, Sleepy!"

"Sleepy" is a familiar Wampum nickname for the Ballplayer. When he was a little boy, Allen was hit in the eye with a tin can, an injury that left his left eyelid drooping slightly. When he made his living playing baseball in major league cities around the country, the nickname would sometimes be picked up and misconstrued by the media to denote laziness. But here, at home, "Sleepy" is spoken only with affection.

"Sleepy!"

The voice belongs to Jim Santelli, one of the Ballplayer's high school buddies and a fellow member of the 1960 Wampum High School championship basketball team.

Allen jumps out of the car, and the two men embrace in the middle of the street.

"We were just talking about you the other night," Santelli tells his friend. "Some kid in Ellwood City just passed you on the top ten all-time scoring list in basketball. They had a write-up in the paper."

Allen smiles. "How many years did the kid play varsity at Ellwood City?" he asks his old high school teammate.

"Four," says Santelli.

"Well, if you'll remember," Sleepy reminds his high

school buddy gently, "back then we could only play three years of varsity ball. But then, who's counting?"

His point made, Allen probes his friend for news of his former high school teammates. They exchange bits of information, but before saying goodbye Santelli wants to make sure Sleepy's writer friend knows all about his former teammate's basketball skills.

He grabs Allen's shoulder. "This guy was the Magic Johnson of high school basketball back when the rest of us were taking one-hand set shots," he tells me excitedly. "Sleepy could stuff one hand, both hands, either hand. He could jump right through the roof. We measured it one time, and it came out that he could touch a spot on the backboard sixteen inches above the rim. He could have been NBA, if it wasn't for the fact that he could hit that little ball so far."

Clearly, around Wampum, Allen is today remembered as much for his skills on the basketball court as for his ability with a baseball bat. Wampum basketball aficionados still remember the time Allen matched up against Gus Johnson, the former NBA great, in a local summer league basketball game. "Dick had this thing against dunking the ball," an Allen friend who played with the Ballplayer in that memorable game tells me the next day. "We grew up as country boys, and country boys don't like to showboat. Then came Gus Johnson and the famous breakaway. We all remember it. Fast break, Dick all by himself, nobody between him and the hoop. He's cruising toward the basket for an easy lay-up when all of a sudden Gus Johnson takes off in the air. As Dick goes up to lay the ball in the basket, Johnson soars up from nowhere and knocks the ball out of his hands. None of us had ever seen that happen to Dick before. After that,

Dick dunked everything. *Everything!* It was frightening to watch."

So deep was his love of basketball that in his early Philadelphia baseball years, the Ballplayer would often spend his off-days shooting hoops with the 76ers, a team that then included the likes of Chet Walker, Luke Jackson, Wali Jones, and Wilt Chamberlain. Once, when Richie Ashburn, the former big league ballplayer-turned-announcer, was asked during a broadcast to name the greatest basketball player he ever saw play in Philadelphia's legendary Penn Palestra, his answer was immediate — Rich Allen.

Back in Big Blue, the Ballplayer is amused by the encounter with his former classmate. "Keeping track of stats and such things is a way of life around here," he tells me. "In that way, Wampum is just like the big leagues, really. Hell, Pete Rose can tell you about every hit he ever had, who he hit it off, what field it was hit to, the kind of pitch it was. That kind of thing always put me to sleep. All I wanted to do was grab a bat and go out and win us one."

The Ballplayer is standing in front of a vacant lot where his boyhood home once stood.

He is in his batting stance.

To get here, the Ballplayer has driven Big Blue across a small bridge spanning the Beaver River into the tiny village of Chewton.

Only a few sticks remain on the overgrown lot where the old Allen frame house once stood. But the baseball diamond, the one built with WPA funds, the same field that would sometimes serve as home grounds for the Homestead Grays and the Pittsburgh Crawfords of the old Negro

Leagues back when the Ballplayer was a little boy, remains right across the street.

"Imaginary baseball," he tells me excitedly. "It's the purest version of the game."

Allen tugs at his shirt sleeves and pushes his cowboy hat down on top of his head, mimicking the same routine he went through whenever he stepped to the plate against major league pitching. He takes a few practice swings with his imaginary bat.

Between his feet, Allen has formed a pile of stones with his boots.

He picks up one of the stones, tosses it in the air, and takes a swing with his imaginary bat.

"As a kid, I used to stand right here," he tells me, "with a broomstick in my hands. When I played imaginary ball, I was always the Dodgers. I would bat stones and work my way through the Dodger lineup — Reese, Furillo, Snider, Hodges — waiting, just waiting, for *his* turn to come around."

Allen pauses dramatically, then cups his hands to his mouth. "Now *battting*," he says, imitating the stadium echo of a public address announcer. "For the Brook-lyn Dodg-ers . . . num-ber four-*tee-two* . . .

Dick Allen reaches down and picks up another pebble. "The Jackie Robinson stone," he says, tossing the pebble in the air and catching it, "was always the one that broke a window."

It's getting dark, and the Ballplayer's beginning to think it might be a better idea to stop, maybe get a couple of beers, and save the trip to Mother Allen's house until tomorrow.

He pulls Big Blue in front of a low, flat building one block off the main drag in Wampum.

The building is a tavern called the Paramount. Inside there is a horseshoe bar, a pool table, a long shuffleboard table, and a jukebox. On the wall is a Pirates schedule, a notice about a ladies softball game, information on the Pennsylvania Lucky Number. A sign on the wall underlines Wampum's economic woes:

NO CONTRACT
NO REAL WAGES
NO REAL JOBS
NO FUTURE, PERIOD
SUPPORT LOCAL 1082

A half dozen shot-and-beer locals sit at the bar.

"Hey, Sleepy."

The greetings come from around the bar.

"Couple of Rolling Rocks," says Allen quietly.

When the bartender goes to get the beer, Allen confides that his favorite beer is really Heineken but that Wampum is an American beer town. "I drink the American beer out of respect for the people who work in the mill," he tells me in a near whisper, "but the stuff kills me."

Relaxed, Allen lights a Kent Golden Light and sips slowly from the cold beer. Our recent stop in front of his old high school is still on his mind. "Only five black kids in my graduating class," he tells me. "Five out of a hundred forty-six. On the surface I was accepted by everyone. My brothers Hank and Ronnie were big basketball stars. Everybody knows Mother. She is loved in this community. Wampum is that kind of town, and the fact that we were all athletes gave us a place here."

Still, the Ballplayer wants the writer to know that growing up black in Wampum was difficult. "Dating was the hardest part," Allen says. "Compared to many places,

Wampum is about as racially tolerant as anywhere I've been. But there were things you just didn't do — and still don't. I could never think about dating a white girl. I had a crush on a girl in my class all four years of high school. I think she felt the same way about me. But it was a hands-off romance. I could never even be seen talking to her, let alone date her. It wasn't that I wanted to go out with white girls. There just wasn't any other color around. When prom time came around, I'd be set up with some black girl from Ellwood City that I didn't even know and didn't want to know."

Two more Rolling Rocks suddenly appear in front of us, courtesy of a shot-and-beer veteran across the bar.

"See, sports was all I had," Allen continues, sipping from the new can of cold beer. "Lucky I had that. My biggest fear growing up here was that I'd end up working in the mills. I used to watch men leave for the mills every day with their lunch pails. They'd put in their eight hours or their ten hours or their twelve hours, and then they'd come home and sit in front of the television with a beer. It used to scare me to see it. Now I come home and I see these same men with fifteen and twenty years of mill work under their belts and they're laid off. What was it all for?"

As the Ballplayer talks, the bar begins to fill up with the very same laid-off workers the Ballplayer has been talking about. Word of Allen's presence in Wampum has seeped through town. Anxious to liven up the proceedings, he goes to the jukebox to find a song to play. He searches hard among the white working-class anthems, finally finding a rap remake of Bill Withers's classic "Lean on Me." He comes back singing.

Some times in my life
we all have pain
we all have sorrow . . .

Another paradox about Dick Allen is that while his image
is that of the bad-ass rebel, his voice is that of a sensitive
tenor. The soft, high voice contrasts starkly with his
powerful physique. Once, in the middle of his playing
career with the Phillies, he even formed his own do-wop
group. He called his group the Ebonistics and made himself
lead singer. The five-person group played in local Philadelphia night spots, once even performing between halves of a
Philadelphia 76ers game at the Spectrum. On that occasion,
Allen entertained the crowd with a feisty version of Archie
Bell and the Drells' "Tighten Up," followed by a slower-
tempoed ballad, "Echoes of November."

The Ballplayer received rave reviews for his musical
efforts. One Philadelphia sportswriter–turned–music re-
viewer wrote:

> . . . here came Rich Allen. Flowered shirt. Tie six inches
> wide. Hiphugger bell-bottom pants. A microphone in his
> hands. Rich Allen the most booed man in Philadelphia from
> April to October, when [Eagles coach] Joe Kuharich takes
> over, walked out in front of 9,557 people at the Spectrum
> last night to sing with his group, The Ebonistics, and a most
> predictable thing happened. He was booed. Two songs
> later, though, a most unpredictable thing happened. They
> cheered Rich Allen. They cheered him as warmly as they
> have ever cheered him after a game-winning home run.

Back at the bar in Wampum, the locals surround Allen.
He has not been back home for a visit in some time, and his
neighbors are eager for news.

While the Ballplayer makes small talk, a man named Ken Johnson introduces himself to me. He is Allen's cousin. He has heard about the book, and he wants to get a few things on the record about Wampum for the writer's consideration. "It's not easy being Dickie Allen and coming home to Wampum," says Johnson after checking to make sure his cousin is out of hearing range. "Everybody wants a piece. When he was making the big paycheck, it was hard for him to know how to act. And it's still that way. If he comes in here and buys everybody drinks, he's a big shot. If he doesn't, he's cheap. Know how he handles it? I buy, then at the end of the night he takes me aside and hands me forty bucks. He buys the house all night, but nobody knows."

Johnson proceeds to fill me in about more Allen folklore, about prodigious home runs he has seen the Ballplayer hit in Wampum sandlots ("One we all remember went six hundred feet, over a railroad trestle. When we saw where it landed, we all fell down on the ground. Six guys started walking it off immediately. Everybody wanted a measurement") and about the dramatic feats he has seen his cousin perform on the basketball courts ("How many guys you know who could thunderdunk in 1960?").

Finally, he asks me if Allen has told me about imaginary baseball.

I tell him about our visit to Chewton.

"Did he tell you about his imaginary horses?"

Huh?

"Oh yeah," Allen's cousin tells me. "When Dickie was a little boy, he had a whole stable of broomstick horses. He had names for all of them too. He could always entertain himself. He was a kid who could be alone, preferred it really. You'd hear him laughing all by himself in the stable.

If Dickie could have played his major league career in empty ballparks — no fans, no media — he would have hit eight hundred, nine hundred home runs. He would have made people forget all about Hank Aaron."

Several tunes on the jukebox and many Rolling Rocks later, the Ballplayer challenges me to a game of shuffleboard, warning me that he's not very good. I accept the challenge and, as he predicted, I take control of the game early. But in the late stages of the game, just as the score reaches 18 to 15 in my favor, Allen grows suddenly serious. He studies the table carefully. With uncanny accuracy, he sends two of the circular weights glistening down the table through the sawdust. Both weights pull up just shy of the table's edge, three-pointers both. The Ballplayer wins, 21 to 18.

Delighted at his come-from-behind victory, Allen breaks into a dance. "In the midnight hour," he sings. "That's when Dick Allen somehow always manages to bail out Richie."

The next morning, Dick Allen steers Big Blue up the long driveway to Era Allen's home. "Not too many people have survived a trip to the reservation," he tells me only half smiling.

These days, trips home to Wampum are less frequent for the Ballplayer. Over the years, the many baseball controversies, his gypsylike wanderings, his taste for beer and love of good times have sometimes made him persona non grata at home, where mother Era Allen still directs the Allen family with a strong and unbending hand.

Perhaps most difficult of all for Mother Allen to accept is her son's divorce from Barbara Moore, an attractive, soft-spoken woman whom he married in the spring of 1963. Barbara Moore remains popular with the Allen clan, as are the three Allen offspring, and their virtual exclusion from the family is still a difficult subject.

This particular trip home is complicated by the presence of a writer. Era Allen has never been one to welcome strangers toting notebooks into her home. "In Mother's view," Allen tells me, "what goes on in the family is meant to stay there. She doesn't believe in talking about things. I had to learn things about my father by overhearing other people talk. Her truth is in the Bible." Mother Allen, her son tells me, simply cannot understand why anyone would want to read about the Allen family when they can read the Bible instead. "Of course, with all that's been written about me," he adds hastily, "it's little wonder she finds more peace reading her Bible."

The night before, over beers at the Paramount Tavern, Allen had tried to explain the special role his mother has played in his life. "Mother has been tough on me," he said. "She never gave me any slack. 'You waste your baseball talent,' she would tell me, 'it's your sin.' But she was always there when I needed her. When I was alone in my hotel room, alone and afraid, I would call and she would tell me, 'Dickie, nothing's going to happen to you. *He's* with you.' Mother would say it with such assurance. My mother has special powers, you'll see. It's a power that works through her faith and prayers."

The Ballplayer tells me the story of the serious car accident that had left Caesar, an older brother, near death by the side of a road in Wampum. The doctors had informed the Allen family to expect the worst. But Era Allen never lost faith. "She went to that hospital every day and read her

Bible to him," he explained. "She would dab his forehead with a cool cloth and repeat her favorite psalms over and over. Slowly, he began to come around. Today, he's one hundred percent."

But the real miracle, Allen tells me, came after his brother's release from the hospital. "Before the accident, brother Caesar was one very bad dude. Strong and bad-tempered. He used to clear barrooms single-handed. One night he was sitting in a local bar when this guy came in and began using the 'nigger' word. Caesar just about tore that place to pieces. But since the recovery, he doesn't drink, he doesn't fight. That's the miracle. He has turned his life over to Jesus. To me it was clear proof of Mother's spiritual powers."

On a more earthly level, Era Allen's powers once also included that of chief contract negotiator. Back in 1959, her son's junior year in high school, the year the big league baseball scouts began seriously knocking on the Allen front door, it was Era Allen who listened and sifted through the offers. The man she listened to most closely was a sixty-six-year-old Phillies scout named John Ogden, a gruff-mannered man with a no-nonsense style who spotted the young ballplayer's athletic gifts early. Over the following two years, Ogden sent many missives to the Phillies, repeatedly describing the western Pennsylvania phenom to the front office as a baseball player "with muscles that can be seen rippling right through his uniform."

In a stroke of scouting genius, Ogden brought Judy Johnson, the former Negro League star, around to Wampum to meet the young athlete. "Even at age nineteen," Allen says proudly, "I was already a budding Negro League historian." For her part, Era Allen was impressed with Ogden's integrity and eventually encouraged her son to sign, but only after she laid down some terms of her own. Ogden got Dick Allen's signature, but in exchange the Phillies agreed to sign Dick's older brothers Hank and Coy to contracts as well — Hank as a player, Coy as a scout. For signing, Dick Allen would receive a $60,000 bonus, the highest ever paid to a black ballplayer at the time.

The Ballplayer pulls Big Blue into his mother's driveway. He gets out of the car and looks down at the long rolling front lawn that runs some hundred yards down to the road. "Don't know about you, but I don't want to be cutting no lawn," Allen says laughing. "If you're smart, you'll keep it moving."

As we come through the door, Era Allen is sitting in a chair watching a soap opera. Despite her attempt to look uninterested in her son's arrival, her eyes betray her true feelings. When she takes my hand, her grip is firm, like her son's. Dick takes a seat opposite his mother and invites me to sit next to her. "Isn't she pretty?" the Ballplayer says to me.

It is more a statement than a question; and in fact there is an inner beauty to Era Allen that radiates through a practiced tough demeanor. At eighty years of age, she wears her full white hair pulled tight to the back of her head, making her appear wise and stately. Her eyes are clear and bright and penetrating. Sitting in her living room, she is surrounded by mementos and trophies of her sons' athletic careers. A large drawing of son Dick hangs on the wall next to the front door. A Bible sits on a nearby table.

Visits home to Mother Allen's have never been easy for Dick Allen. Strict about her Bible, Era Allen believes in following God's word — no drink, no smoke. While son Dick has followed in his mother's footsteps in accepting the message of Jesus Christ, the specifics that go along with that message have always been difficult for the Ballplayer. "You wouldn't know it to watch me," the Ballplayer explained before our trip, "but I have a strong religious belief deep within me. In my worst days in baseball, I have felt the Lord alongside me. Without Him, I never would have been able to stand in against all the abuse."

In the days before our trip to Wampum, Allen tried to articulate the childhood pain he felt growing up. "My father left our home for good when I was fifteen," he said. "He and Mother had their differences. He would come home from work and want a drink after a long day. But Mother would absolutely forbid it. But my dad was his own man. Nobody could tell him how to live. When he couldn't take it anymore, he left. After that, he lived about thirty miles up the road in Coraopolis. He had his own trash-hauling business. He began with one truck, then built it to six trucks, all on his own. He loved horses and always kept them around, which is how I learned to love them, too. My dad was only five feet eight, but he was the toughest man I'd ever met. He was totally without fear. If there was a dog waiting for him when he went to pick up a trash load, he would fix it with a look that would scare the poor animal half to death. One time a Doberman made the mistake of coming right at him. He lifted that dog in the air with one quick shot to the jaw. After that, the owner said the animal was no good as a watchdog. He had to put him to sleep."

Allen told me that his father's desertion was difficult on his mother. "Money was always our biggest concern," he recalled. "We boys would go out and play ball, while Mother would sit in the rocking chair and sew torn clothes for the neighbors to make a few dollars. I think that her insecurity about money was part of the reason she was so tough on us. She was particularly tough on me, but I guess I needed it. I always was rebellious. I liked doing things my own way, like my dad, I guess. I look at pictures of myself as a boy and I see a lot of sadness. I never could understand why Mother and Dad couldn't get along. When my dad died, I wanted to find out more about him, but it's impossible to bring up his name around home. I try to tell Mother I'm not asking about her husband, I'm asking about my dad. But it's a subject we can't talk about."

Now, in Era Allen's living room, the Ballplayer excuses himself. His brother Caesar is working on a tractor motor in his mother's garage. He wants to see if he can help.

When the door to the garage closes, Era Allen turns to me. "Do you have brothers and sisters?" she asks me.

"Six," I tell her. "But I lost a brother recently to cancer. He was twenty-three."

Mother Allen's eyes grow soft. "I recently lost a daughter," she tells me. "She had been sick for a long time. I still feel the pain. I always will."

Having found safe ground, Era Allen proceeds to tell me of her other children and their children, her grandchildren. She tells me how much she misses her two daughters who live in California and how proud she is of Dick's children. She then tells me about Barbara Allen, Dick's ex-wife. "She is a devoted mother," Era Allen says proudly. "The children — all three — are educated and well mannered. She did good by them."

What is most important to Era Allen is the First Baptist Church of Wampum, the religious center for seventeen black families in nearby Chewton. The church, she explains, has been the center of her life since its dedication in 1922. "I've tried to raise all my children on God's word," she tells me. "Some of my children have followed His laws better than others. Dick, I could never get to church. Even today, every New Year's Eve, we have a Watch Night service at our church. We recite passages of the Bible. The boys can't make it home anymore, but Ronnie and Hank call me and we have a service right over the phone. But not Dick. I tell him, 'Live the life you want, but remember you'll be standing before the Lord come Judgment Day all by yourself.'"

Sensing an opening, I ask Era Allen about Dick's formative years. "As a little boy, Dick was the most bashful one in the family," Mrs. Allen tells me. "He would stay real close to me, clinging to my dress. He was always real quiet — sensitive, the most sensitive of all my boys. He liked to be alone a lot. He was always batting stones. I remember, because I was the one paying for new window panes all over the neighborhood. The neighbors wouldn't even bother to ask the kids who was responsible. They would just come and tell me it was Dickie again. I knew they were right, too, because there were no baseball fields in all of Chewton or Wampum that could hold a stone if Dickie hit it good."

As for her son's big league years, Era Allen tells me she could never understand the fuss. "It was all so hard to figure out. The sportswriters, especially. They would ask me the dumbest questions. They always wanted to know how I felt being the mother of a star. I was never the mother of a star. That was just my boy Dickie out there. The star business I had no time for."

Era Allen leans over and looks at me closely. "I used to tell people who asked me questions about Dickie one thing," she says in a near whisper, "and now I'll tell you the same thing: Dickie was born to play baseball. That was what he was put on this earth to do. If you had seen him as a little boy, the way I did, batting stones all by himself for days and days, pretending he was every player in the Dodger lineup, you'd know, the way I know, that it was a special calling."

By the time Dick reenters the room, it is time to end our visit.

"I'll be home again soon," the Ballplayer tells his mother, kissing her cheek softly.

"I don't believe you, so don't say it," Era Allen scolds her son.

Before leaving, I shake Era Allen's hand. She grips my fingers tightly. "Your brother's in peace," she tells me.

Outside, Big Blue waits. We decide to get a couple of cold ones.

•4•

On the Whole . . . Philadelphia

Dick Allen on the Philadelphia years, 1964–1969:

No baseball season in my fifteen-year career had the highs and lows of '64. I was the National League's Rookie of the Year, but I made over 40 errors at third base. The fans in Philadelphia booed me right from the start, and then at the end of the season they actually had a "Richie Allen Night" for me. The Temps said it best baby, I was a ball of confusion.

It's still hard for me to accept that we had a six-and-a-half-game lead with only twelve games to go. Yet when I look back at all the teams I played with, the '64 Phillies bunch stands out in terms of my affection. That team will never be listed among the great teams in baseball history. But, man, could we gig! In the outfield, we had Wes Covington, Tony Gonzalez, and Johnny Callison. Around the infield, guys like Tony Taylor, Cookie Rojas, Ruben Amaro. On the mound, Bunning, Short, Mahaffey, Wise — Baldschun in the bullpen. We were long odds to finish in the money that year, and we just missed.

To this day I can't set foot in Philadelphia without somebody asking me about the Phillies' collapse of '64. The people of Philadelphia still want an explanation. The truth is, I don't have one. I've never blamed Gene Mauch for breaking the normal pitching rotation near the end of the season. At the time, pitching Jim Bunning and Chris Short with only two days' rest didn't seem like such a bad idea. Short and Bunning were our two aces, and Gene had every reason to believe they would come through for us. To second-guess Mauch afterwards is too easy, and I never was able to think like a sportswriter.

The problem with Gene Mauch as a field general in 1964 — and it haunted him to his retirement — was that he held the game too tightly in his hand. Mauch is a brilliant strategist. I learned more about baseball as a chess game under Gene Mauch than I did from anybody else in baseball. The man's a master of the little game — when to bunt, how to steal a sign, what base to throw to, all the ways to outthink your opponent. But Gene Mauch never let us play the game instinctively — and without that you can't win enough baseball games to capture a flag.

During the '64 skid, I went to Mauch with an idea. I'd been working with Clay Dalrymple, our catcher, on a pickoff play at third base. Runners were getting too big a jump off third base — believe me, I know. I was right there watching it. So together we went to work on a play where I would sneak behind the runner at third and he would gun it down to me at the bag on the beat of three. We worked out a complex series of signals so the runner would be caught off guard.

I told Mauch we wanted to try the pickoff play the next time we saw a runner leaning too far off third. Mauch shot it down on the spot. All he could see was the ball bounding

out to left field. He couldn't see how a play like that could
ignite the team. For him, the risk wasn't worth it. I
thought it was just what the '64 Phils needed to start playing the game with confidence again. We had been playing
out of fear for too long.

As it turned out, one of the most disastrous games of that
whole '64 collapse came with two weeks left in the season.
We're playing Cincinnati. Two outs in the sixth inning, and
we're locked in a scoreless tie. Chico Ruiz on third, Frank
Robinson at the plate. Suddenly Ruiz takes off. He's stealing home! Nobody could believe Ruiz would steal home
with Robinson at the plate. Guys on the Reds were scream-
ing "No, Chico! No, no!" But he was gone, baby, and he was
safe. We lost that game 1–0, and it broke our hump. It was
the start of our ten-game losing streak.

Now I'm not saying that Dalrymple and I would have
chosen that very moment to try to pick Ruiz off third. But
maybe we would have, or maybe we would have tried it
earlier that week and hearing about it Ruiz would have had
more respect for our ability to keep him tight. Point is, we
needed to play more daring. If we had, things would have
begun to happen.

Once we really started to skid, Mauch became a wild
man. After losses, he would close the clubhouse door and
start dressing us down, throwing things around. Callison
and I would look at each other and try not to break out
laughing. After one particular loss in that ten-game streak,
Mauch stood up on a table in the clubhouse and began
telling us what a good marriage he had and how for the
good of the team we should all follow his lead. I think
maybe Gene lost it at that point. There wasn't a guy in that
clubhouse who gave a damn about Mauch's marriage. This

wasn't a morality campaign. It was a pennant race. All we wanted to do was start winning again.

No team in baseball history worked harder than the '64 Phillies. By season's end, we were on the verge of exhaustion. The last two weeks of the season, Johnny Callison was sick and white as a ghost. He shouldn't have been out there, but there was no getting him out of the lineup. I remember one game near the end of the season, Callison drew a walk and could hardly make it down to first. He just sort of stumbled down the line. Mauch started to send somebody in to run for him, but when Callison saw that, he started waving him off. Tough sumbuck, that Callison.

Things came to an emotional climax for me the night of September 25 — "Richie Allen Night." The night was organized by a group of Philadelphia Jewish and black merchants. The Phillies front office was totally against the idea. One, we were losing our grip in the pennant race. Two, Phillies general manager John Quinn told me the club didn't believe in having special nights for rookies.

Before the game that night, I was presented with a television, snow tires, luggage, and a stereo. It may not sound like much now, but at the time I was making $10,000, and those gifts were much needed. The group also contributed a $1,000 scholarship for my daughter Teri's future education. What I remember best about that night was looking at my mother sitting in the stands. She was so proud of me. I told her after the game that all those days of cutting class at Wampum High to play ball had finally paid off. She didn't buy it. Unfortunately, that special occasion in late summer '64 only proved a diversion from the ongoing disaster that we were going through as a team.

Things got very quiet on the Phillies bench during the

final weeks of the season. Mauch was wrapped so tight that we were afraid to open our mouths. It was hard for me, being a rookie, to know how to respond. In some respects, because I was having such a good season, I was the natural team leader. But being a rookie, I was also expected to maintain a low profile. It was hard to speak up with Mauch. One of Mauch's nicknames was the Little General — and for good reason. To try to assume team leadership with Mauch around would have been like a buck private trying to overrule General Patton.

All we needed in the final weeks of '64 was Mauch to pat us on the fanny and say, "Thanks fellas, good effort, we'll get 'em tomorrow." Instead, we got ranting and raving, and all that did was make us feel more tired than we already were. I can't blame Gene totally. He was only thirty-eight years old, and he wanted to win so badly. He would have done anything to win. He and I were a lot alike in that way. I respect him for that. But somewhere along the line in '64, and maybe it was because he had such a frustrating career as a ballplayer himself, Gene Mauch forgot the most elementary rule of baseball: to have fun.

We never could get it together in '65. The Phillies front office was in a state of panic all season. The nightmare of '64 got everybody focused on keeping their jobs instead of winning ballgames, and I mean *everybody* — from Mauch to general manager John Quinn to the players on the team. We lost the scrappiness that got us so close in '64.

To show they could act decisively, the Phillies went out and got Dick Stuart and Bo Belinsky. To me, this was proof that we were on the fast track to oblivion. In my book Stuart and Belinsky were baseball novelties. Stuart hit 28

home runs for us in '65 but batted only .234. Worse, Stuart
was the kind of guy who would hit a home run, and then
want somebody to run out and measure it. They called him
Dr. Strangeglove because he couldn't field a lick. And
Belinsky — all he really wanted was to get his picture in
the New York papers with a different blonde every week.
He won four games for us that year. In 1964, we were a
cohesive team; now we were a baseball club. Mauch used to
look around the clubhouse and shake his head in disgust. I
couldn't blame him.

After the Frank Thomas fight in early July, I started
playing angry baseball. It seemed the whole city of Philadelphia blamed me for what happened. They hung banners
from the bleachers at Connie Mack Stadium in support of
Thomas. I began getting hate mail, and lots of it. Most of
the letters I got started off with "nigger." None of the
letters was ever signed. Racists are cowards. I learned this
from my days in Little Rock. After a while I just dumped
the mail in the trash, unopened.

Things happened after the Thomas fiasco that I'll never
forget. One night I came in from third base to the dugout in
Connie Mack Stadium and saw a guy holding a little boy up
in the air with one hand and pointing at me with the other.
He was teaching his son to boo me. In my mind he was also
teaching his son to hate.

Another time I was going through the tunnel that led
from the dugout to the clubhouse when some guy reached
through the crowd and hit me with a sucker punch that
caught me in my side. I went back out, but there were
dozens of people hanging over the railings and I couldn't
find who did it. I couldn't take on the whole ballpark. All I
wanted was for someone to step forward and call me a name
to my face. I was ready to take somebody out.

What burned me most about the fans in Philadelphia was the hypocrisy. One night shortly after the Thomas fight, I came to the plate with the bases loaded in a game against the Giants. It was a Thursday twinighter and there was a huge crowd, almost 40,000 people. The fans were particularly rough that night. Back in those days, doubleheaders were dangerous in Philadelphia. Give Philadelphia fans two games to get drunk, and anything could happen.

That night there was a particularly hostile group sitting near third base. One guy kept yelling "darkie" at me and getting big laughs for it. Another guy sitting in the same section kept shouting that Richie Allen should go back to South Street with "the rest of the monkeys." Back then South Street was where all the brothers hung out in Philadelphia.

At the plate, I could feel the anger ripping through my veins. First pitch, I hit a shot off Jack Sanford that went out of the park just to the left of the old Ballantine scoreboard in right-center. I got all of it. I circled the bases quickly behind the other three runners, my head down as always. When I touched home plate, I looked around and saw the crowd on their feet — 40,000 Philadelphians were giving me a standing ovation. The roar was deafening. Thirty seconds earlier I was a monkey from South Street. Now I was a hero. It was the ultimate mind game, and it was my mind they were playing with.

After the Thomas incident, I had trouble at home, too. There were threatening phone calls day and night, and they were always racial in nature. Barbara would pick up the phone and a voice would tell her not to expect me home that night. One night a car drove up on our lawn and spun its wheels, tearing up the grass. I came home from the park late after one game and there was garbage — chicken bones — all over the front lawn.

Once it was clear that the Phillies were not going to be a contender, I began concentrating on my fielding. In '64, third base was a brand-new position for me — and it showed to the tune of 41 errors. In '65, I made only 26 errors, and that was with Dick Stuart over at first base. I still was capable of throwing the ball into the first-base box seats. But less often. I was beginning to like it over at the hot corner.

I finished the '65 season with a .302 batting average, 20 home runs, and a renewed confidence about playing third base. But as a team, where it counted, we finished in sixth place. As bad as the collapse of '64 was emotionally, finishing out of the money like this was far worse.

One of the few things that gave me pleasure right through the Philadelphia years was my love of the horses. I've always had horses around me. As a kid, my dad kept a few old horses behind our house in Chewton. I'd grown up knowing how to care for them and how to ride them. The best thing about horses is that they take on the personality of the people who care for them. I always liked my horses because they were independent, like me. I fed my horses well and gave them a lot of exercise, and in return they performed. If Mauch had given me the same respect I gave my horses, things may have been different.

But Mauch hated the fact that I loved the horses. He saw it as a distraction from baseball.

In fact, horses kept me in the game. If we were in Philadelphia for a home stand, I'd get up at 5:30 or 6:00 in the morning, saddle up my horse Blaze and head for

Philadelphia's Fairmount Park for a brisk run. It would get me up for that night's game. The Phillies front office was always afraid I'd fall off and get hurt. If they had seen what I was doing they would have had something to really get upset about. Every morning four or five of us horse lovers would meet and race through the park. And I mean race, baby! We turned Fairmount Park into our personal Preakness.

We ran like the wind, but I was never afraid of getting hurt on Blaze. We were in constant communication. I knew exactly what he could do, and he knew exactly what was expected of him. With things beginning to go so bad in my baseball life, I used to fantasize on those rides what life would be like as a jockey. Here was a sport I would have loved. Nothing except you, the horse, and the competition. Here I was blessed with this big strong physique and all I could think about was how happy I'd be in a small man's body.

After coming so close in 1964, we slipped out of the race for the next five seasons. The closest we came was fourth place in 1966. With each frustrating run for the pennant, things began to deteriorate between me and the Phillies front office. Inside, all I could think about was winning one, and we kept getting further away. Off the field, at contract time, the Phillies would try to use the team's place in the standings against me.

Not surprisingly, owners will take any edge they can. I was hip to that. As far as contract negotiations go, I was always big league. I had learned from the best negotiator around — my mother. We would sit down — my mother, my brothers, and I — after every baseball season and go over what I had accomplished. We would consider my stats and also — and this was an important one — what the team drew in attendance that season. If I was going to have to live with those headlines, then I was going to get compensated for the people that those headlines brought into the seats. Together, we would arrive at a number that we felt was fair.

After my rookie season in '64, I told the Phillies I wanted $25,000 for the '65 season, a $15,000 raise. We settled for $20,000.

In '67, I asked for $100,000 and settled for $85,000.

In my early Philadelphia years, I negotiated with John Quinn, then the Phillies general manager. Quinn's negotiating style was to dismiss my requests out of hand. After a while I began dealing directly with Bob Carpenter, the Phils owner. I liked the Carpenter family. Both Bob and later his son Ruly — who owned the team in the seventies — were gentlemen. But the Carpenters were wealthy, part of the Delaware Du Pont family, and that in itself made it hard for them to know this poor black kid from Wampum. Baseball owners know black players come from unstable backgrounds, and either consciously or not — and in the case of the Carpenter family I truly believe it was unconscious — they often use that insecurity against them at contract time.

When I came up to the big leagues in the sixties, many of baseball's black stars were from the South, from the fields of Alabama and Tennessee, and they were vulnerable to high-pressure tactics. I remember the first time I met Willie Mays, he said, "What part of the *old* country you from, boy?" To black ballplayers the "old country" meant Dixie. When I told him I was from Pennsylvania, he was impressed. I think Mays detected that I was bringing a new attitude to the game. Like all black players, he was always happy to see a new day dawning.

At contract time, the standard line from owners was to pay your dues first and the real dust will come later. It's a lie. In baseball, as in life, you've got to get what's coming to you while you're producing because the day you stop — it's later, baby.

In my case, having grown up in western Pennsylvania among white people, I could walk that walk, talk that talk. Contract time, I had my act together. A jacket and tie, always. I would state clearly what I had done the season before. Front office types weren't used to dealing with black players who could talk their game. When I came in for meetings at contract time, the boss men would perspire right through their sport jackets.

The Phillies learned early that if I wasn't happy I would hold out. I never thought about staying away for a week or two — I was willing to miss the entire season. There were times when I was with the Phillies that the idea of playing industrial league ball in Wampum sounded a lot better than spending another year back in the lion's den. In the end, the Phillies knew that as far as Dick Allen was concerned, leaving the big leagues was always an option. It was a hell of a trump card.

As for the fans in Philadelphia, they resented my attitude about money right from the start. I always believed a man should get every cent he's worth — whether he's delivering Krimpets from a Tastykake truck or trying to hit that little white ball for a living. Back home in western Pennsylvania, steel mill country, people seemed to understand why I would hold out until I got what I wanted. People back home were used to getting the money they deserved, and if they didn't, they'd strike.

But in Philadelphia, their attitude was that I should be grateful just to be allowed on the field. The sportswriters there would make things worse by comparing my salary to other players in the league that had been around longer. But that's not the way I did business. Dick Allen set his own standards. I thought Philadelphia would look up to me for being an individual. Instead it became one more thing for them to dislike about me.

The most frightening moment in my life came on the evening of August 24, 1967, in Philadelphia. We had just been rained out against the Pirates. I found myself home with a rare night off. I was killing time around the house, bored, no ball to play, so I went outside to start up my old 1950 Ford. Not surprisingly, the car wouldn't kick over — it always did have problems starting in the rain — so I released the brake and began giving it a push. The car was on a hill, with the front wheels wedged against the curb. To move it, I had to shove it from the front. I gave it a push, but when I did my foot slipped on the wet ground. I felt my right hand rip through the headlight.

When I pulled out my hand, it looked like it had been blown off by a land mine. Blood was spurting everywhere. Underneath the blood, my hand looked like a bowl of spaghetti. My mother was staying with us at the time. When I walked into the house and Mother saw what happened, she ran to the bathroom, soaked a towel in water, and tied it around my arm above the wound. How she knew to do that, I'll never know. Like I say, my mother has always had special powers. The towel acted as a tourniquet, and I know now that she saved my life.

On the way to the hospital, all I could think about was what a horrible end this was to my career. When I arrived at the hospital, a doctor cleared the blood away and found two three-inch cuts on my hand and another on my wrist. Glass from the headlight was still sticking out of the wound. I had severed two tendons and the ulnar nerve on my right hand.

The doctors decided to operate. While I was waiting for surgery, one of the doctors asked me for an autograph, and another guy tried to shake my hand — classic Philly-style. They took me into surgery, and five doctors worked on me for five hours. When I came out of it, the chief surgeon told me the bad news. He said that full recovery with this type of injury occurred in less than half the cases. In any event, it would be six weeks before any recovery could be determined. They put my arm in a cast up to my bicep. I was finished for the '67 season.

Right away, my accident took on dark and mysterious overtones in Philadelphia. Nobody, it seemed, wanted to believe the real story. Over the next few days I heard all kinds of crazy versions about what happened: I'd been knifed in a bar fight, I'd been cut with a razor by a jealous lover, I had jumped through a window after getting caught sleeping with a teammate's wife. Maybe I brought all the speculation on myself by dodging the press. Or maybe the fact that I liked to have a few drinks made the other stories seem possible. Whatever the reason, I was depressed enough by what happened. The fact that people didn't believe me only made it worse.

The people who knew me well — and not many people in Philadelphia did know me well — knew I was telling the truth. I've always liked old cars, ever since I was a boy in Wampum. Even today I like to throw up the hood of Big

Blue and tinker. I still keep an old VW at my mother's house in Wampum. First thing I do when I go home is get under the hood of that baby and get it purring. Some people collect baseball memorabilia for a hobby. I change my oil.

The sportswriters in Philadelphia could have helped that situation by looking at the facts. Even had they not believed me, they should have figured I could never tell a lie — not with my mother around. Instead, they fueled the speculation. If I had lied about what happened that night, my mother would have made sure the doctors had a whole lot more to work on than a ripped-up hand.

When the cast finally came off, I was shocked at the extent of the damage. They had placed two steel pins in my hand — one across the hand and the other through the wrist. There was an eight-inch scar that ran from the outside of my hand to the middle of my wrist. I could move my little finger and my ring finger, but barely. My baseball future looked very shaky.

Following the Phillies' '67 season, I took off on a solitary road trip. I needed to find myself. Things with Barbara weren't going well. In the best of circumstances, it's difficult to play baseball and maintain a relationship. I was away from home so much of the time. When I'd come home, I'd have to adjust to being a husband and a father. In my case, I had the additional worry of looking after my wife and daughter down at the ballpark. The way the fans were going after me, anything seemed possible. Barbara liked going to the park to watch me play. But the boos were harder on her than they were on me.

Mostly I wanted to get away from the Philadelphia writers and the other cynics. I went on a serious bender. I drove to California, then through Mexico, and I found that being alone gave me peace of mind. After a while I stopped drinking and began to work at healing my hand.

All during that trip, I carried a piece of foam rubber that I had taped into the shape of a ball. I squeezed that baby constantly. I squeezed it in my car, in bars, even in bed. When I woke up in the morning, I would start squeezing it all over again. There wasn't a waking minute that whole fall and winter when I didn't have my hand wrapped around that piece of rubber. I was determined my career was not going to end with a freak accident.

When I got to California, I looked up Willie Davis, the Dodgers ballplayer, and asked him to go to a local playground with me. I needed to take some hitting. Willie would throw me soft lollipop pitches, and I would swing at the ball nice and easy. When I hit the ball solid, I was fine. But when I hit the ball off the end of the bat, it would send a shock right through my whole body. It was like hitting your crazy bone, only the crazy bone felt like it ran through my whole body.

When I got back to Philadelphia late that winter, I signed on with a construction crew where a friend of mine was the foreman. I began laying bricks — hundreds of bricks a day. Every time I picked up a brick, my hand hurt. But the tough outside work was just what my hand needed. After a while I began enjoying the work, too. It was nice to do a job and not hear boos while I was doing it.

I left for spring training in Clearwater, Florida, early that '68 season. I had a lot to prove. Before the headlight accident ended the '67 season for me, I had been having a different kind of Dick Allen season. As a team, we weren't going anywhere. At the time I was greatly influenced by Wilt Chamberlain. Wilt had just changed his game dramat-

ically, going from dominant scorer to team player. Instead
of taking it to the hoop, he dished off more, and the team
had begun winning — and winning big — because of it.

In '66, I had hit .317 with 40 home runs. Forty round-
trippers and where did we finish as a team? Fourth place. It
got me to thinking that if I adjusted my game a bit in order
to showcase some of the other stars on that '67 team — Bill
White, Johnny Callison, Tony Taylor, Tony Gonzalez —
maybe it would make a difference. I sacrificed myself more.
I made them pitch to me and began taking more walks. I
was less the big bad bat in the lineup. But while I was
trying to play a different kind of game, my fielding slipped
again. In '66, I made 9 errors at third base. In '67, I made
35 errors. The experiment was over. I was going back to
clout ball.

On my way to spring training, I drove past one of those
coin-operated batting ranges. I took a leaded bat and a golf
glove out of the trunk of my car and went into the cage. (I
discovered in California that wearing a golf glove gave my
fingers some support. Later that season, other players in
the league started wearing golf gloves at the plate too. I
think they thought I was starting a fashion trend.) That day
at the cage I think I missed the first twelve balls. But then
I started to get loose, and as I did the ball started to travel.
I never felt so happy in my life. I stayed in that cage for
hours knocking the ball around until blisters started form-
ing on my hand and I had to quit. I went back to that cage
every day for a week after that. I didn't have much feeling
in my hand, but it didn't seem to matter.

When I was convinced that I was able to hit the ball again
big league style, I got on a plane and went back to Philadelphia to consult with my doctors. I was afraid that may-

be I was working the hand too hard. The Phillies took this as a sign that I was AWOL. When I got to Philadelphia, I saw the headlines again: ALLEN MISSING IN CLEARWATER. Here I had gone to Florida early after spending the whole fall and winter working that hand back into shape — and this was the thanks.

When the '68 season opened, Mauch started me in left field. I could hit all right, but I couldn't throw. On fly balls, our shortstop — Roberto Pena — would hustle out to left field to be my designated relay man. It wasn't ideal, but I was beginning to feel like everything was going to be all right.

But the fans in the left-field bleachers at Connie Mack Stadium had other plans. Apparently, they had already made up their minds about both the Frank Thomas incident and the headlight injury. They began arming themselves. At first they threw pennies at me, then big bolts, and finally beer bottles. I began wearing a batting helmet in the outfield for protection. For the rest of my career, I wore that helmet while playing the field.

Luckily, a lot of guys on the club kept me loose that season. The guys on the pine took one look at me wearing that helmet in left field and broke up. They started calling me "Crash Helmet" — which later got shortened to "Crash" — another name I didn't need.

On June 23, 1968, the Phillies fired Mauch. The writers claimed I went to Phils owner Bob Carpenter and gave him a "Mauch or me" ultimatum. That never happened. The truth was that Mauch's spirit had been broken. He *allowed* himself to be let go. The fact that the team was no longer winning made the game a burden. I felt the same way. I've always respected number 4 for that. The game is meant to be won.

My relationship with Mauch went through many changes over the four and a half seasons I played under him. When I first began playing for Gene in '64, I liked him. He had a way of building up my enthusiasm. He used to gather all the writers around and tell them how important I was to the team. He knew it would get back to me and put pressure on me to deliver. It was good psychology.

Mauch was also a fighter — and I liked fighters. At 5'10" and 165 pounds, he was well defined. He was only in his late thirties when I joined the team, but he looked and acted like he could handle himself with anybody. I saw a lot of players, bigger and younger, back down from Mauch in arguments. He had a way of fixing you with those steely eyes, never giving an inch. Scared the hell out of most guys, but usually I found it amusing. Mauch may have been a scrapper, but he didn't want to scrap with no Dick Allen. We both knew that.

In the early days, I felt that Mauch genuinely liked me. He would come into the clubhouse and treat me as an equal. I used to appreciate that until I realized he never talked to any of the other players on the team. I didn't want special treatment. With my reputation, I couldn't afford it.

After the '64 collapse Mauch put his arm around my shoulders and told me how proud he was of me. He said, "You and Johnny [Callison] never choked. You took the heat. I wish I could have fielded nine players just like you two." I was annoyed that he was knocking other guys on the team. When Mauch turned his back, I put my hands to my throat in a choking gesture. Callison saw me and busted up. Like I said, I've never blamed Mauch for what happened. But lots of other players did. They couldn't understand why Mauch didn't bring up Ferguson Jenkins or John Boozer from the farm to give our starting pitchers a blow. But Mauch never did like working with the young talent — and he wasn't much good at recognizing it either, particularly in Fergie's case.

I first began losing respect for Mauch after the Thomas fight. As far as I was concerned, things would have been different between me and the Philadelphia fans had Mauch handled that situation differently. Thomas hit me with a bat. A month or so after the Thomas thing, Juan Marichal hit Johnny Roseboro with a bat at home plate and they damn near ran Marichal out of baseball. But in my case Thomas's decision to use his bat as a weapon was *under*played. Instead Mauch silenced me with the threat of a fine. In all my years in baseball, the only time I ever let a fine stand in the way of doing what I thought was right was after the Thomas fight. It was a lesson hard-earned.

By the '68 season I had my mind on only one thing: getting the hell out of Philadelphia. Near the end of the '67 season I'd gone to Bob Carpenter four or five times and asked to be traded. He refused. He kept telling me that things would turn around. I didn't believe it. The fans were no longer just booing — it was open warfare. I had security people checking my mail, which was almost always nasty and usually threatening. Some of my teammates suggested that I hire protection. My family was scared and unhappy. And the Phillies had become a lousy team. I wanted out.

I decided to get myself traded. This time the double standard would work in my favor. I began to set my *own* rules. Before ballgames, instead of going straight to the ballpark, I started making regular stops at watering holes along the way. I had a regular bar route from my home in northwest Philadelphia to the ballpark in the inner city. I stopped at black joints and white joints — I was an equal opportunity drinker — but usually only for a beer at each stop. I used to fantasize chartering a bus to the ballpark for fans via my new route. The Dick Allen Baseball Bar Tour. Would have made it fun for everybody, too. I found some great baseball fans along the way — Dick Allen fans, too. I had my admirers, I guess, but they sure didn't sit within earshot of me at Connie Mack Stadium.

Whenever Mauch would smell booze on my breath, he'd throw a tantrum. "Richie," he'd say, "since you like to drink so much, those beers you had before you got here will cost you a grand." I wouldn't even flinch. "Skip," I'd say. "Let's make it two grand — that way I can get a taste on the way to the park tomorrow, too."

I'm no psychiatrist, but I believe that it was during those '67–'68 seasons that I first began to act the role that Philadelphia had carved out for me. I'd been hearing I was a bum for so long that I began to think maybe that's just what I was. I began to hit the sauce pretty good, and I didn't care who knew it.

By the second month of the '68 season, Mauch and I were no longer communicating. By now he was fining me almost every week: $1,000 for drinking, $500 for missing batting practice, $1,500 for showing up late for a game. Sometimes the fines would be announced; most times they weren't. My weekly fines were the equal of some players' paychecks.

Mauch couldn't stand piloting a losing team. He would come into the clubhouse after a loss and throw things around at random. He even began to talk rough with me. We were coming to a showdown, even though we both knew it would be a one-round affair. When he called me lazy in front of the other players one night, I knew he'd gone too far. He left himself no room to back off. Everybody was waiting for the explosion. He *had* to leave. He was too smart to let Richie Allen get in his face.

Just days before Mauch was fired, I had gone to see Carpenter again. I told him that all the stories in the press about the coming showdown between me and Mauch had made me a depressed and confused ballplayer. In my mind, I told Carpenter, it was no longer a question of wanting to be traded — I *had* to be traded.

Again, he refused. Instead, he told me that Mauch was going to be fired. I pleaded with him the same way I had pleaded with Mauch after the Thomas fight. I kept saying the same words to Bob Carpenter over and over again. *Let it be me.*

No, Carpenter said. His mind was made up. He told me that Mauch had been his manager for eight years. Except for 1964, he explained, the Phillies had never been in the chase. It was time for a change. He told me that Bob Skinner was going to take over. I didn't know much about Skinner except that he had been a fine ballplayer.

"Make a fresh go of it, Rich," Carpenter begged me before I left. "You can still call Philadelphia your home."

The season after Mauch left Philadelphia, he was hired as manager of the Montreal Expos. Shortly after he arrived in Montreal, a sportswriter asked Mauch what he would do if he was managing Rich Allen today. Mauch said, "I'd find him, fine him, and play him; find him, fine him, and play him — just like I did when I was managing the Phillies." The quote was picked up and got lots of laughs around the baseball world. But to me it was just more proof that

Mauch never did understand Dick Allen. Gene Mauch could never control me with fines. He would have been better off just trying to know me.

On June 24, 1969, I got caught in a traffic jam trying to get into New York. At the time I owned four thoroughbreds with some friends. That day I had had a horse running in the third at Monmouth. We were scheduled to play a twinight doubleheader against the Mets, and at the last minute the starting time of the game had been changed. I was late. Guilty.

On my way to Shea Stadium I switched on the radio and found out that Bob Skinner had suspended me. One of the promises Skinner had made to me was that he would never take any action against me without hearing what I had to say first. Not that I had much to say. I wanted to be traded. I was unhappy. He couldn't deal with that. Nobody could. That was the problem.

When I heard the news on the radio I remember thinking, Goodbye baseball. It's hard to describe my state of mind at that point in my life. I was twenty-seven years old and I felt unloved, unappreciated, and unbelievably confused.

Instead of going to the ballpark, I went back to my hotel room in New York and packed my bag. What had me most upset was that Skinner had suspended me without even hearing my explanation. I didn't have one, but I expected him to keep his word. He had already fined me $1,000 in early May for missing a plane to St. Louis. I was too far down the line. It was getting hard for me to remember a time when I liked playing baseball.

At the time Skinner suspended me, I was hitting .318 with 19 home runs and 45 RBIs. I'd been playing in a state of frenzied anger. It used to amaze even me that I could be so productive in my state of mind. I would stand in at the plate and gather all my frustration for one big swing. Judging by how far some of the balls were sailing out of the park, I had a lot of frustration.

In the meantime, the Phillies had moved me over to first base. I liked playing first base. At third, I could scoop the ground ball, but I never did find the right groove for the throw across the diamond. In the minors, I had played shortstop, second base, left field, and center field. The Phillies moved me to left after I dislocated my shoulder in the '66 season. Put me there again in '68, the season after the headlight injury. But at first base I felt at home. I could concentrate on making the good play. I'd watched Bill White play the bag for years and had picked up a lot of tricks from watching him. It was strange to be hitting well, playing a position I liked, and still be feeling so miserable.

At the time of my suspension, the Phillies were in deep trouble as a team. Three of our best players — Tony Taylor, Deron Johnson, and Johnny Callison — were out with injuries. Rick Wise was in the army reserve, Chris Short was out for the season. If we had been a contender, maybe things would have gone a different way. But as it was, I was determined I would never play another baseball game in a Phillies uniform. Quinn and Skinner thought I would come back from the suspension with my tail between my legs. The suspension was costing me $450 a day — and with three young kids, the loss of money hurt. But like I said before, I had made up my mind that no fine — no matter how stiff — would ever dictate my behavior again. Instead of begging to come back I decided that until the Phillies traded me, I was officially in the horse business.

During the suspension, I cut myself off from everybody, even my family. No newspapers. I began spending my time on farms in Maryland and Virginia looking for horses to buy and race. I stayed with a friend for a few weeks in a hunting lodge in Gettysburg, Pennsylvania. The sportswriters were tracking me as though I were a mass murderer, but I covered my tracks well. *If Dick Allen doesn't want to be found, there's not a man in this or any other world who can find me.* I wasn't sure I could make the same money in the horse game that I made in baseball, but I knew I'd be happier.

Finally, I did call my mother. She was the one person I couldn't cut off. She begged me to talk to Clem Capozzoli. Clem had been acting as my agent for three years. He wasn't an agent in an official capacity. Clem actually worked for the American Baking Company in Philadelphia. Sportswriters used to call him my surrogate father, and I suppose he was. He had a way of calming me down and putting options I could deal with on the table. Clem never took a cent from me. He wouldn't let me give him anything. I loved Clem, and that's why I hadn't called him. I knew he'd want me to return to baseball.

But when Mother asks me to do something, I usually do. I called Clem. Clem begged me to return to baseball. He put it on a highly personal basis. "For me, Rich," he said. "I've never asked you for anything before. But you were born to play baseball. You owe the world your talent." My mother worked on me the same way. "Dickie," she said, "it's a sin not to use your talent."

Over the next few days, Clem spoke with Bob Carpenter about reinstating me. Then Clem called me and asked if there was anything I wanted to communicate to Carpenter.

Just one thing, I told Clem. Tell him to get me the hell out of Philadelphia.

Finally, in mid-July, I met with Carpenter at a suburban Philadelphia restaurant. He was very straight with me. He told me how much I meant to the team. He said the team needed a leader, and I could be the one. He told me that Skinner was prepared to forget about the whole thing.

I said, "Mr. Carpenter, you *have* to trade me."

He told me that he couldn't trade me right away because the June trading deadline had passed. Then he said, "But Rich, you have my word — following the 1969 season, you'll never play another game as a Philadelphia Phillie." Then he said, "But if you say one word to the press about this I'll deny it — and all bets are off." Bob Carpenter's word was good enough for me. I met with Skinner the next day and was reinstated on July 20 — after 26 days, 29 games, and $12,000 in lost pay.

That afternoon, when Skinner met with the press and was asked about the reinstatement, he said, "There's no way I expect anybody to be a new person." Minutes before in a private meeting he'd told me he expected me to be just that. I knew then that Bob Skinner had a game face and a media face. I was going to have to be careful.

First time up after the 26-day suspension, I lashed a double to left-center that scored us a run in Houston. Standing on second, I burst out laughing. They could do a lot to this ol' country boy from Wampum. They could take my money, take my freedom, take my self-esteem, but they couldn't take my stroke.

The first week of August, I began writing messages in the dirt around first base. I called it dirt-doodling.

I started doing it one night after some guys in the seats behind first base in Connie Mack Stadium began waving bags of hash at me. They were calling me "hashhead." Things were so weird by this time that nothing surprised me. When I got out to the bag, I wrote the word HASH in the infield dirt with my spikes.

The fans loved it. I liked it too. It was a way of talking back creatively without having to talk to the newspapers. The next night, I wrote PETE. Pete Cera was the Philadelphia clubhouse man. He'd been clubhouse man when I was in Little Rock, and we were very close. I had promised him a dedication.

I was beginning to have fun again. The next night I wrote BOO — that was my personal greeting to the Philadelphia fans. Then I scrawled OCT. 2, my day of liberation, the last game of the season, my last game as a Phillie.

The big laughs came on the night of August 3 when I doodled the word LEE with my spikes in front of the first-base bag. I had been joking with Lee Weyer, the first-base umpire, for a couple of nights. I always had a good rapport with umpires. I'd never been thrown out of a game in my whole career. I respected the men in blue. Weyer, in particular, seemed to appreciate my approach to the game. I was breaking the boredom for him in what was a meaningless series in what had become a meaningless Phillies season.

The next inning, Weyer took a turn doodling himself, spelling out the words RICHIE ALLEN #15 just inside the first-base line.

"Lee," I said. "You know I hate being called Richie."

Weyer laughed and then very carefully erased the RICHIE part from his artwork.

Everybody was enjoying my doodling except John Quinn, the Phillies general manager. Quinn complained to Bowie Kuhn, the baseball commissioner at the time, and to Warren Giles, the National League president. Between innings of a game later that week, I was told to cease and desist. That inning I wrote MOM, because nobody told me what to do except my mother, and NO, just to make my feelings known. The next day one of the Philadelphia papers printed a copy of the First Amendment and accused the baseball establishment of censorship. It was one of the few times I found the newspapers on my side.

Shortly after that, I moved my things out of the Phillies clubhouse and into an adjacent storage room. The press said I thought myself too important to dress with the rest of the players on the team. But the real reason I did it was to keep my teammates from getting in trouble. I had become baseball's bad boy, the bad ass of the National League, and I didn't want any of the players to get into trouble for associating with me. Johnny Briggs was one of my best friends on the team, but by separating myself I could keep him at arm's length — at least in public. I didn't want him or anybody else to be found guilty by association.

On August 7, Bob Skinner quit. His resignation came after I decided not to play in an exhibition game against our farm team in Reading, Pennsylvania. For Skinner, it was the final straw.

"You're coming with us, Allen," he yelled at me when I told him of my plans to miss the game.

I explained to him that Bob Carpenter had given me permission to miss the exhibition. He thought I was lying.

He went to Carpenter and was told I *had* been given permission to skip the game.

As far as I was concerned, Skinner was a quitter.

Skinner was an old-school baseball man and resented the fact that I had a relationship with Bob Carpenter. He thought it undermined his authority. But my relationship with Bob Carpenter had been going on for six years. Nobody, outside of my family, knew more about what I had gone through in the Phillies organization. Carpenter was more than an owner to me. That doesn't mean that he always condoned my behavior. "You've got to grow up," he'd tell me. I'd say, "I did grow up, black and poor. You grew up white and rich. But we're both grown up."

Skinner never understood my time in Philadelphia. He never felt the boos, the abuse, the threats. There were times when I wanted to sit down and talk to Skinner. I had been with the Phillies for a lot of years. I could have helped him understand the way things worked. But Bob Skinner wanted me to be just like everybody else. I *wasn't* like everybody else. I'd hit 40 home runs in one season for the Phillies. I'd hit over .300 for four seasons. I'd been to hell and back.

The Phillies named George Myatt, our third-base coach, to finish out the season as manager. At the time, we were 44–64, buried in fifth place, 24½ games out of first. Myatt's first words to the press on being named manager were about me: "I don't think God Almighty Hisself could handle Richie Allen, so all I can do is try."

When I heard that, I walked up to him and said, "George, you don't 'handle' people, you treat them. Horses, you handle."

On September 28, 1969, I played my last game at Connie

Mack Stadium as a Phillie. There were only 6,000 people in the ballpark. All of them, it seemed, had come out to boo me one last time. I suppose it was only fitting that the final sounds I would hear in that ballpark were the same ones I'd heard as a rookie six years earlier. When the final out was made I looked up to the grandstand and gave the boobirds a final big wave. I gave the first-base sack a friendly pat and then kissed the palm of my hand and rubbed it in the infield grass.

I was free.

•5•

Scenes from a Summer Season: 1987

We're in St. Louis, Ballplayer and writer, for the first in a series of Old-Timers' exhibitions that the Ballplayer has consented to play in this summer.

The three-inning exhibitions (which precede regularly scheduled major league games) are sponsored by Equitable Insurance, and $10,000 in proceeds from each game goes to BAT, a fund for down-and-out retired ballplayers. Allen has agreed to play in the games because of the fund and because he is tentatively testing the baseball waters again to see if there's a place for him in the game he loves.

There is ambivalence on the Ballplayer's part about playing in these games. Despite the good cause and the stipend provided by Equitable, Allen remains convinced that he never really did retire from baseball in 1977, but rather that baseball left him. Besides, he doesn't feel like an old-timer.

He has donned a uniform only occasionally in the decade

since his playing days, most notably for a brief spring training stint with the Texas Rangers in 1982 and again in 1985 when he served as a roving minor league hitting instructor for the Chicago White Sox. He liked working with young hitters but disliked putting on a baseball uniform. To Dick Allen, a baseball uniform is a sacred cloak, meant only for guys who take the field to play.

But now that he is in St. Louis and on the field among his own, his ambivalence toward playing in this particular exhibition vanishes. During batting practice, he jokes easily around the batting cage with the St. Louis Cardinals of his heyday — Curt Flood, Lou Brock, Bob Gibson — gibing them all good-naturedly as they take their swings. Nothing makes the Ballplayer happier than being around the sounds of baseball.

When the former Cardinals finish their turns in the batting cage, Allen (who is playing against the Cardinals on a mixed team of National League Old-Timers) steps into the cage himself. Suddenly the happy sounds of baseball cease. When Dick Allen is taking his cuts, batting cages become as quiet as libraries, so profound is the respect among his colleagues for how hard he hits the ball. The Ballplayer doesn't disappoint. He slashes several balls to center, then drills one effortlessly into the left-field stands.

Following batting practice, there is the introduction of the Old-Timers roster. As the names are introduced, the players trot out, wave their caps, and line up along both base lines. That completed, there is a pause, and then an announcement is made that a special guest is in attendance. The special guest is Cool Papa Bell, one of the great stars of the old Negro Leagues. Allen, a self-styled aficionado of Negro League baseball, often tells the story of how Josh Gibson, another great star of the Negro Leagues, used to boast that Cool Papa was so fast he could get out of bed, turn out the lights across the room, and be back in bed under the covers before the lights went out.

Cool Papa, now eighty-four, emerges gingerly from the shadows of the St. Louis dugout and waves to the crowd. Surprised and moved by the sight of the nattily dressed old Negro Leaguer, Dick Allen steps away from the third-base line and vigorously cajoles his Old-Timer teammates into sustained applause.

The three-inning exhibition moves along briskly, the highlights coming when Allen scorches a base hit to left field and later when Lou Brock, the former Cardinal speedster, steals second base cleanly. Following the out that concludes the three-inning affair, Allen grabs his glove and streaks across the field to catch up with Cool Papa Bell. As the other players skip past hurriedly to get to the clubhouse, the two black ballplayers stand in the tunnel talking softly.

Afterward, Allen is buoyant recalling the conversation. "He said I could have been one of them," the Ballplayer says of Cool Papa Bell. "He said I had power and I could run, the two most important requirements in Negro League baseball." It is a rare display of Dick Allen braggadocio. Later, reflecting on his encounter with Bell, Allen waxes philosophic: "It's funny. Back in their day, the Negro League players all wanted to be big leaguers. They felt deprived because they could never get in. And there I was, in my day, a big leaguer who felt like he lost out because he never got a chance to play in the Negro Leagues.

* * *

Hollywood, California

It's late afternoon, and we're sitting in a small North Hollywood restaurant, one of the Ballplayer's hangouts, an unprepossessing little joint run by two sisters from Thailand.

The television is turned to WTBS, Ted Turner's Atlanta superstation. The scheduled Braves game is currently in a rain delay, and in the meantime the station is showing extensive footage of baseball stars from the sixties and seventies. There are clips of Joe Morgan, the former Reds second baseman, making plays in the field and standing in at the plate, a shot of Fergie Jenkins, the former Cubs left-handed pitcher, and yet another of Orlando Cepeda, the onetime Giants slugging first baseman.

The Ballplayer looks up without interest.

When the show breaks for a commercial, the Ballplayer speaks. "I'm going to prove something to you," he says in a monotone. "Ten bucks says you don't see that kid Allen on the screen."

When the film clips resume after the commercial break, there is more footage — Juan Marichal, Mickey Mantle, Early Wynn, Don Drysdale, Willie McCovey, Manny Mota, Roger Maris, Maury Wills, Ernie Banks, Willie Horton, Lou Brock. As the individual highlights flicker on the screen, a voice-over encapsulates each player's career.

Suddenly, up on the screen, there appears a still photo of a young black man wearing heavy black glasses and a red and white pinstriped baseball uniform.

The voiceover: "In 1964, Richie Allen was named the National League Rookie of the Year. In 1972, he was named the Most Valuable Player in the American League."

That's all. No film clips, no detailed highlights of the ballplayer's career.

"Well, I guess I'm wrong," the Ballplayer says. "Or would you say I'm only half wrong?"

The Ballplayer sips his beer in silence.

"You see," he says several minutes later, "a lot of people are under the impression that I have no time for baseball. But the truth is, baseball really has no time for me."

Washington, D.C.

The writer has a headache, dry mouth, runny eyes. The reason for the big league fatigue is Lew Burdette, the former Milwaukee Braves pitcher. The night before, the Ballplayer and the writer merely meant to stop by the hospitality suite of the Washington Marriott for a quick visit.

Who was to know that Lew Burdette would be holding court?

The reason for the Washington visit is the annual Cracker Jack Old-Timers game in Robert F. Kennedy Stadium. Over the years, the game has developed into a minor classic for baseball fans. Unlike the Equitable Old-Timers' Series, this is a full nine-inning game and is broadcast every year by one of the major networks. The ball game draws many Hall of Famers — Aaron, DiMaggio, Mays, and so on — all of whom appreciate the national exposure and the chance to catch up with old friends.

The Ballplayer has agreed to play in the Cracker Jack game this season for the first time.

Burdette was killing time all by his lonesome when the Ballplayer and the writer walked into the room. Spotting the old Braves pitcher, Allen, a great fan of the old Milwaukee Braves, seemed to have just seen a vision.

"Burdette, you tough old bird!" Allen said, greeting his old rival.

Burdette, now in his early sixties, his face craggy with long summer lines from his eighteen years of standing in the sun on major league pitching mounds, stares hard at the Ballplayer. Finally, recognition crosses his face.

"Oh shit! Richie Allen. My worst nightmare." He says this right to the Ballplayer. "You and your kind are the reasons I hung 'em up."

Over his eighteen seasons in baseball, Lew Burdette compiled 203 lifetime wins before retiring in 1967. At the time, Dick Allen was only in his third major league season. But Burdette remembers the Ballplayer well. "Yeah, you and that big-ass bat of yours scared the piss out of me," he says, shaking Allen's hand.

Allen is still laughing. "Maybe, but my face is still wet from all that spit you globbed on the ball," he tells Burdette.

The rest of the night, the Ballplayer and Burdette lapse into stream-of-consciousness baseball talk — blacks in baseball, the lively ball, Henry Aaron, life in the big leagues. While the big league bullshit and big league beers flow freely, the writer listens to the former and (unfortunately) keeps pace with the latter.

Finally, near four in the morning, both ballplayers are finally ready to call it a night. On the way up in the elevator, Burdette begins to go to his mouth with his fingers. Allen catches on immediately.

Imaginary baseball.

When the elevator doors open, Allen steps out and assumes his batting stance.

Burdette, still standing in the elevator, goes into his wind-up. Allen is clawing at the carpet with his boots. Just as Burdette comes down with his long right arm, the elevator doors close.

Now there is only the writer and Burdette riding the elevator in silence. Alone, the writer can't resist asking the former pitcher a question.

"Lew," I begin cautiously. "How did you get away with that spitter all those years?"

Burdette fixes me with a pitying look. "You dumb ass," he says. "What the hell are you talking about? I never threw no goddamn spitter."

When the elevator doors open, I make a quick exit.

Fourteen hours later, with the Old-Timers' game about to start, the vision of watching Burdette go through the motions of loading up a spitball in the elevator of the Washington Marriott has dimmed, submerged beneath five cups of coffee, a light lunch, and a handful of aspirin.

But then all the writer has to do is watch the game. Dick Allen, the Ballplayer, has to play in it.

Allen is batting fourth. Second pitch — bang! — a 400-foot-plus home run to straightaway center.

After the game, I ask the Ballplayer how he managed to hit a home run after such a hard night. "Hank Aaron came to me during batting practice," he explains, "and told me the fences were moved in for the game. He figured we should have no trouble popping one over. Well, I didn't want to hit no short-fence homer, I wanted to nail it. Hell, you should have seen what I did to Burdette's spitter last night. That sucker's still in orbit."

Levittown, Pennsylvania

Dick Allen is signing autographs at six bucks a throw. The occasion is a baseball memorabilia show, one of two the Ballplayer has contracted to do this summer. Baseball memorabilia is big business, and Allen is receiving a healthy fee for his scribblings. Still, he finds these shows depressing. He never did like signing autographs, and even today when he is asked for his signature the Ballplayer is more apt to extend his hand and say, "If you don't mind, I'd rather not — but it sure is a pleasure meeting you." He has always placed more value on a firm handshake than a signed piece of paper.

He has agreed to do these autograph shows for the money, but now he is paying the price. The people who line up for his autograph are more collectors than fans, and there is little in the way of personal interaction. Most ask the Ballplayer to sign baseballs or baseball cards, and they instruct him on the kind of pen to use and where specifically to sign. Their interest is resale value.

At this show, the lines are long, Philadelphia, the site of Allen's most controversial days, being only a few miles away. There is little to break the inherent monotony.

"Dick?"

A young couple stands in front of the Ballplayer.

"Uh-huh?"

The man holds up a child, no more than two years old.

"I want you to meet Richard Allen."

The Ballplayer looks up.

"We named him after you," the young father says.

Dick Allen touches the baby's hand. "After me?"

"Yes sir."

The Ballplayer is moved. "Listen here, Richard Allen," he says to the baby, smiling, "don't you worry what name they call you — just make your parents proud."

The father beams.

When the couple walks away, the Ballplayer excuses himself, saying he needs to take a short break.

*   *   *

In 1963, the Phillies sent the Ballplayer to Little Rock, making him the first black ballplayer in Arkansas history. "I was scared," recalls Allen, "scared and alone."

In the midst of the famous Phils collapse of '64, a group of merchants threw an impromptu "Richie Allen Night." "The Phils were against the idea," recalls the Ballplayer. "They didn't think a rookie deserved such an honor."

Allen with wife Barbara and daughter Teri in 1964, after being named the National League's Rookie of the Year.

Following a well-publicized fight with Frank Thomas in 1965, Phillies fans made it clear whom they blamed for the incident. Allen never told anyone his side of the story.

The Ballplayer had a small but ardent cult following in Philadelphia. Here, an Allen contingent in the left-field bleachers looks for their hero to play clout ball.

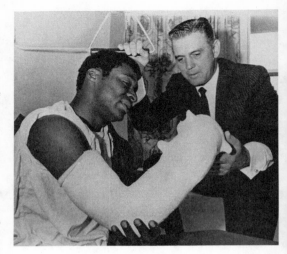

Right: The Ballplayer explains to Phils manager Gene Mauch how his hand went through a headlight as he tried to push his stalled car outside his home in 1967. Mauch believed his story; many Philadelphia baseball fans did not.
Below: The Ballplayer calls Bob Gibson the meanest pitcher he ever faced in baseball. Says Allen: "He would knock you down and then meet you at home plate to see if you wanted to make something of it."

Above: In 1969, his last season in Philadelphia, Allen began writing messages in the dirt around first base. Recalls the Ballplayer: "The fans loved it, the ballplayers loved it, even the umpires loved it—but it got the front-office types uptight." *Right:* Following his last game as a Phillie in Connie Mack Stadium, the Ballplayer threw kisses to the fans. "I was glad to be leaving that house of doom," he says.

During his playing days, the Ballplayer would often fantasize life as a jockey by leading wild romps through Philadelphia's Fairmount Park on his horse Blaze.

Cover photographs like this one, which appeared on *Sports Illustrated* in 1972, helped solidify the Ballplayer's image as a baseball outlaw.

The Allen family (left to right): brother Ron, Era Allen, brother Hank, Chuck Tanner, and the Ballplayer.

Allen received a hero's welcome upon his return to Philadelphia in 1975. "So much had changed," he recalls, "it was like playing in a different city."

Philadelphia, Pennsylvania

We're sitting in a South Philadelphia tavern and restaurant — Allen, the writer, and two members of the Veterans Stadium grounds crew that the Ballplayer befriended during his Philadelphia playing days.

The All-Star game is on. Allen, who never watches baseball on television, has been persuaded to stop and watch a few innings. But by the second inning, he is already bored. Watching baseball on television is not his kind of fun.

Instead, he wants to sing. Back in his playing days, he would often harmonize before a game in the clubhouse with the grounds crew to get loose. He is a fan of do-wop music.

At the moment, he is teaching me how to sing streetcorner style. He instructs me to push the little part of my ear against my eardrum with my index finger. When you harmonize, he explains, it's important that you only hear the sound of your own singing voice.

The Ballplayer is singing lead, circa late 1950s:

> Gosh knows I love you
> Heaven knows it's true
> I want to be near you

As the Ballplayer croons, his companions harmonize in the background.

> Do-wop-eee-do
> Boom-ba-boom-boom-ba
> Do-wop-eee-do
> Boom-ba-boom-boom-ba

When we finish, the South Philly patrons give us a nice round of applause.

Inspired by our performance, three South Philly guys decide to give the Ballplayer and his back-ups a little competition. After huddling for a few minutes, they stand next to their bar stools and begin singing a vintage fifties tune by the Moonglows.

> Sin-cere-ly
> Don't you know that I love you?
> I'll do anything for you
> Just say you'll be mine

The Ballplayer is impressed. "Listen, fellows," he says to us. "This is getting serious. We need a song that will blow these chumps out, dig? We need a tune that has meaning. The way to win in this kind of thing is to hit them where they live."

One of our grounds crew back-ups has an idea. After a quick huddle and rehearsal, the Ballplayer is ready to sing lead.

> As I walk into this world
> Nothing can stop
> the Duke of Earl

In the background, fingers pressed to our ears, the Ballplayer's back-up singers harmonize.

> Duke, Duke, Duke
> Duke of Earl
> Duke Duke
> Duke of Earl

Duke Duke
Duke of Earl

The three South Philly guys now are the ones who are impressed. While the All-Star game flickers on the television across the room, they spend a long time talking among themselves, searching desperately for a strong comeback. Finally, they come out of the huddle. When they do, they begin singing a relatively obscure early-seventies hit that was made popular by the Intruders, a Philadelphia rhythm-and-blues group.

I'll always love my Momma
She's my favorite girl
I'll always love my Momma
She brought me in the world

The Ballplayer can't believe it!

"Owwwweeeeee," he bellows, mimicking James Brown at the height of his frenzied best. "They got us, fellows! We can't beat a song about Momma! We've been scorched in extra innings!"

The Ballplayer walks around the bar to congratulate the victors.

When we finally leave the South Philly restaurant hours later, the Ballplayer doesn't even bother to ask who won the All-Star game.

Philadelphia, Pennsylvania

Dick Allen is standing in a suburban Philadelphia batting cage under the noonday sun. In a few days, he will participate in a home run–hitting contest against fellow

retired ballplayer Greg "The Bull" Luzinski, a former
Phillies teammate and long-ball specialist. The contest is to
be held in Philadelphia's Veterans Stadium between games
of a Phillies-Dodgers doubleheader. In recent days the
Philadelphia media have reported sightings of Luzinski
taking batting practice at the stadium.

The Ballplayer deems such batting practice silly —
though in recent days he has begun stopping at public
coin-operated cages like this one to practice his stroke. At
the moment, however, Allen is disgusted with this particular batting cage setup. For starters, there are only
aluminum bats, which the Ballplayer loathes, and rubber-
coated baseballs, equally loathsome. Worst of all, the balls
do not come in fast enough. Allen stands in the cage and
swats effortlessly at the 70-mph balls that come out of the
machine. There is no challenge.

Suddenly the Ballplayer has an idea. He walks up to the
pitching machine and plants himself about three feet in
front of where the balls come out. As the balls spring out of
the machine, he blasts them right back, snorting angrily.
He does this to twelve balls in a row, banging the machine
at near pointblank range with a barrage of nasty line
drives. When he is finished, he is sweating profusely. And
laughing. "I guess I wanted that machine to remember the
day Dick Allen stopped by," he says, tossing the aluminum
bat into a barrel, his warm-up for the Greg Luzinski
showdown complete.

Philadelphia, Pennsylvania

Circus time, the Ballplayer calls it — Dick Allen against
Greg Luzinski, home run contest, Veterans Stadium. The
rules are simple: seven innings, three outs an inning, everything's an out except a home run.

Last season Luzinski went one on one with Willie Stargell during a similar promotion and won. Never considered a complete ballplayer, Luzinski made his baseball living hitting the long ball — 244 home runs lifetime. His forte: a smooth, easy swing and plenty of weight to put behind it. The Phillies are calling this "The Bull-Blast Shoot-out."

To prepare for tonight's contest, Luzinski, age thirty-six, has worked hard. He has shown up at the park every day for batting practice. He has worked out. He has taken weight off. While waiting for the contest to start, he limbered up vigorously with calisthenics.

To prepare for tonight's contest, Dick Allen, age forty-five, has spent a rough night playing pool with cronies. He's been learning to play pool for the past six months, picking up games where he can in his favorite spots in California and Pennsylvania. He reports an improved pool shooting eye but confesses a need to work on better shot selection.

When the first game of the doubleheader concludes, Allen is introduced to the large Philadelphia crowd and gets a standing ovation. He is glad he didn't come out for the contest in a Dodger uniform. He was tempted to, just to tweak the hometown Philadelphia crowd.

First up, Allen. Two home runs, one upstairs, one a low line drive that whistles down the left-field line and just clears the fence.

Luzinski, however, proves to be stiff competition, as he belts two of his own in the first inning.

It goes like that, dead even, through seven innings. Finally in the eighth, with both ballplayers exhausted, Luzinski, who gets to bat last, breaks the deadlock, winning the competition 8 to 7.

Back in the clubhouse, exhausted, the Bull and Allen embrace. "I told you you'd get tired," Luzinski tells the Ballplayer.

"You're right, Bull," Allen tells his former teammate, mimicking Sylvester Stallone's Rocky. "Give me a rematch, will you? Give me a title shot? Next year I'm going to train harder. I'm going to take it serious. Next year, no out playing pool until two o'clock in the morning for this man. No way. Next year, midnight latest. What do you say, Bull?"

Souderton, Pennsylvania

Lunchtime in Biggie's Place, one of Dick Allen's favorite hangouts, located in a rural Pennsylvania town thirty minutes outside of Philadelphia.

Biggie's Place is a vintage Dick Allen stomping ground: jukebox, pool table, hot roast beef sandwiches and deviled eggs at the bar, a jukebox crowded with country-and-western tunes. On this particular weekday, a handful of senior citizens and working men, most of whom know Allen, sit around the bar over roast beef sandwiches and bottles of beer.

At the moment, the Ballplayer has decided that things at Biggie's Place are too quiet. He goes to the jukebox, and when he sits back down, the strains of Frank Sinatra belting out "New York, New York" fill the room.

His buddies at the bar can't believe it.

Sinatra?

"What? You don't like Frankie?" says Allen to the faces around the bar.

The Ballplayer gets off his bar stool and begins to croon along with the jukebox.

If I can make it there
I'll make it anywhere

As he sings along, he begins dancing, kicking his legs higher and higher, as if in a chorus line.

It's up to you, New York
New York!

When he finishes, the guys at the bar explode into applause. The Ballplayer laughs and then launches into a knowledgeable monologue comparing the great crooners of the fifties, finally proclaiming Tony Bennett the best of the lot. His choice launches a feisty debate among the bar patrons, some choosing Sinatra, others Mel Torme, yet others agreeing with Allen's choice of Bennett. The Biggie's Place lunch crowd has come alive. The Ballplayer has sparked another rally!

Wampum, Pennsylvania
We're sitting in the lounge of the Beaver Falls Holiday Inn, the Ballplayer and the writer. We've taken this late-summer trip to Wampum to visit with several of Allen's friends and acquaintances whom we missed the first time around. It is getting late, the lounge is near empty, and the Ballplayer is reminiscing about his social life in Wampum.

He is telling me again about high school. Specifically, he is talking about his high school sweetheart, the white girl he could never date. "It's hard enough having a crush on a girl," he says sadly. "But when you have a crush on a girl that the town won't let you date, it eats you up."

The Ballplayer has an idea. Maybe, for the purposes of the book, understand, he should call the girl, who still lives in Wampum, and ask her to join us. Maybe she'll help you understand a few things, he tells me.

Thirty minutes later, the Ballplayer's high school crush shows up. She is forty-five years old now, divorced, a mother of two. She has retained a youthful quality, however, and it is easy to picture her as a perky high school student in 1960.

"Here she is," Allen announces. "As pretty as ever."

The Ballplayer's former high school crush sits down, but before she can even get settled, Allen is teasing her.

"You're looking at one of the best cheerleaders in western Pennsylvania history," he says to me.

The Wampum woman blushes.

Allen gets up from the bar and stands next to the woman. "Here's how she used to do it," he tells me. He puts his hands on his hips.

> Ready, set, let's go!
> Sleepy, Sleepy, he's our man.
> If he can't do it, nobody can!

Allen the Ballplayer has become Allen the cheerleader. Not content to stop there, he implores the woman to show the writer her old moves. Reluctantly, the woman does an abbreviated version of the cheer Allen has just demonstrated. The Ballplayer is ecstatic. This is his kind of fun.

Minutes later, Allen excuses himself and I ask the woman about their high school romance. "No, no, it could never have been that," she tells me. "We could never be alone. We only talked to each other when other people were around us. We couldn't even take a friendly walk home from school together."

When the Ballplayer returns, I tell him that maybe I'll call it a night and give him a chance to talk over old times with his high school classmate.

"No, no, no, you stay here," he says quickly.

"Don't you want time alone to catch up with each other?" I ask him.

"No, you don't understand," he says impatiently. "You can't leave us sitting in here alone. You still don't get it? That doesn't go in Wampum."

•6•

Dick Allen, Straight Down the Middle

The following dialogue is based on conversations with Dick Allen, the Ballplayer, over an eighteen-month period.

The Writer: The only baseball books that seem to make it big these days are those that tell all.

The Ballplayer: I can dig. But what do those books say about life? Nothing. So you get your name on the bestseller list. Then what? You've broken the ballplayer code. You're nothing. You ask a question about my life, I'll answer you straight down the middle. You ask me the same question about a former teammate, nothing. I don't give it up.

The Writer: Straight down the middle, did you do drugs when you played ball?

The Ballplayer: Cocaine, no. Greenies, they made me sick. Grass, I've tried it. Booze, guilty.

The Writer: Lots of baseball people tell stories of how Dick Allen would occasionally show up a bit glazed over . . .

The Ballplayer: True, it happened. I'd have a couple of Canadian Clubs and water in the clubhouse before a game.

I would get loose. The white ballplayer would get his head up with a greenie. I got mine up by having a couple.

The Writer: The sportswriters wouldn't write about it?

The Ballplayer: They began to. When they did, I switched to brandy and coffee. They actually thought it was plain coffee.

The Writer: How about during the game?

The Ballplayer: When I played for Philadelphia in the seventies, the Phillies had bathrooms right off the dugouts. One of the guys around the park would put a beer in the towel dispenser for me. I could find a cold green one there in the third and seventh innings — and the fifth inning, too, if we were winning.

The Writer: Nobody ever knew?

The Ballplayer: Yes, guys knew. To my way of thinking beer is better for you in very hot weather than either Gatorade or water. Beer you sweat out. Water makes you go to the bathroom. Gatorade makes me gag.

The Writer: As for grass . . .

The Ballplayer: Not the kind of thing baseball players like to hit on before a game. Imagine getting high and then stepping in against a Bob Gibson or a Juan Marichal. Is there a more frightening prospect?

The Writer: Off the field?

The Ballplayer: It was usually a writer or a photographer who would have smoke. I blew some joint riding cross country with guys like that. Not the daily beat writers, dig? The magazine guys. The amazing thing is that afterward their work would always be right on. They would have insights, and they would get the facts right. I was impressed.

The Writer: It wasn't a regular thing to have a smoke?

The Ballplayer: In my early baseball years, I was a rank

amateur. One night I smoked a big doobie with a buddy and a teammate in a Chicago hotel room just before leaving to get something to eat. We got off the elevator on the wrong floor, silly like kids. We kept stumbling into each other. Somehow, we ended up walking onto a stage where a man was giving a lecture to a large group of doctors. You should have seen their faces when they saw these three giggling brothers walk out onto the stage.

The Writer: Greenies, of course, are a baseball institution.

The Ballplayer: True. Some guys pop them like aspirin. Like everybody else, I did too. Not only did they make me sick to my stomach, they made me angry. If I gulped a couple of greenies and then went to the plate against a pitcher who wasn't throwing strikes, I'd want to go out to the mound and get him. Greenies bent my system out of shape.

The Writer: Why are greenies the baseball drug of choice?

The Ballplayer: Look at the baseball lifestyle — the schedule, the air travel, the hotel life. It defies description. Ballplayers get sick from the water, from the food, from being in the air. Take anybody from civilian life and make them go through a 162-game schedule — without even making them play the game itself — and see what it does to them. Greenies give you a false sense of stamina. They take away that run-down feeling. But when guys stop taking greenies, their bodies crash. It isn't said much, but what becomes important to the ballplayer is staying regular.

The Writer: How did you keep your system together?

The Ballplayer: I had certain rituals, and I didn't deviate from them and still don't. In the morning, I drink V-8 juice, as much as I can stand, with lots of lemon, and two Theragran vitamins. I eat only one meal a day, usually dinner. That meal I eat right. Steak or fish, raw vegetables, a baked potato. In between, of course, I've been known to down a couple of cold ones. But when I feel my stomach needs special fortification, I gulp a special health drink that I blend myself.

The Writer: Which is?

The Ballplayer: I hate to give it up, but here it is, the Dick Allen secret to a healthy stomach. You need the following ingredients:

> Vanilla ice cream (2 scoops)
> 2 raw eggs
> Powder protein (1 Tbsp.)
> Honey (1 Tbsp.)
> 1 banana
> Peanut butter (1 tsp.)

Throw it all in a blender. The result is a protein-packed drink that will keep your system in good running order. It tastes like a milkshake. You won't taste the raw eggs.

The Writer: Sounds like a health drink that could put some weight on.

The Ballplayer: When you're on the Dick Allen program, you have to do 25 sit-ups a day, every day. If you do that, it'll pass right through you.

The Writer: They didn't have Nautilus during your time in baseball?

The Ballplayer: They did, but you couldn't get me near that stuff. Baseball is a fluid game. It requires grace every bit as much as brawn. You need to be in touch with your body. You need to know what it can do. Bulking up gives

your body an unnatural strength. Your mind loses touch
with how your body operates.

The Writer: Who were the baddest cats in baseball?

The Ballplayer: Two guys come to mind. First, Alex
Johnson. Alex played thirteen seasons in the big leagues,
hit .329 in 1970 for the Angels. Why was he so underrated?
Why was he traded so often? Why don't you hear his name
today? I'll tell you why. Because he called everybody "dickhead."

The Writer: Dickhead?

The Ballplayer: To Alex Johnson, baseball was a whole
world of dickheads. Teammates, managers, general managers, owners. Everybody was a dickhead to him. We understood. That was just his way. But it scared the front
office guys to death. They'd walk into the clubhouse to say
hello, and Alex would say, "How ya doin', dickhead?" Just
like that. The front office types would take it personally.
But then again, maybe Alex hit a nerve.

The Writer: The other baddest cat in baseball?

The Ballplayer: Jimmy Ray Hart, the third baseman for
the Giants. I call him "Crow." Back in '62, Crow and I were
competing for a batting championship in the minor leagues.
We were dead even going into the last game of the season
and playing against each other yet. The night before the
game, I invite Crow out for a few drinks. I figure if I get
him sauced enough maybe I can get an edge. So we go out
to a little joint in Williamsport, Pennsylvania, and I throw
a twenty-dollar bill on the bar and tell him we ain't leaving
till the twenty's gone. Remember, this is 1962, a twenty-
dollar bill went a long way then. Crow doesn't say nothing.
He just takes out a big old pack of Pall Malls, throws them
on the bar, and orders up a shot of Old Grand Dad. All night

we drink, and when we finally use up the twenty, Crow reaches in his pocket and throws down his own twenty. All he says is "Let me return the favor."

The Writer: As for that batting title?

The Ballplayer: Next day, I go to the park, all hung over. First person I see? Old Crow, he's out at third base fielding ground balls. Gives me a big wave and a loud hello. When he does that, I make up my mind to have myself a good game at the plate, hangover or no. Comes the game, I go four for six. Crow, he goes six for six. I end up at .329, but he wins the batting title by a couple of percentage points. After the game he comes over to me waving a twenty-dollar bill and asking me where I want to go to celebrate. Let me tell you, Jimmy Ray Hart was one bad man.

The Writer: Why does baseball have such a hard time dealing with free spirits?

The Ballplayer: They don't — only with the black free spirit. Baseball had no problems with Jay Johnstone, or Tug McGraw, or Rick Dempsey, or the Mad Hungarian, or Bo Belinsky, or Casey Stengel. These guys become characters, write books, and are thought to be good for the game. Black ballplayers who go their own way get nailed. They said Alex Johnson was surly. But when Alex played with the Phillies, he would come to my house all the time and play with my kids. He'd put them on his shoulders and give them rides all over the house. One day a guy who worked around the ballpark called the clubhouse before a game and said his car had broken down on the expressway. Alex immediately jumped in his car and drove out to help him. He came back an hour later, still in full uniform, grease up to his elbows. Now, I have to ask myself, is this man a mental case, or is this a man I want as my friend? Alex just wanted to be left alone to play baseball.

The Writer: No matter what you did, it made headlines.

The Ballplayer: Bill White, the great first baseman and one of my old roomies, used to tell writers that Rich Allen never did anything more than anybody else in baseball, it was just that he got caught. And that was true. I cared about winning baseball games. Man, did I care. But the other stuff, that was my business. If I wanted to have a few beers after a game, if I wanted to carry on, nobody was going to tell me not to. I was doing a man's job, making a man's salary, I could make my own decisions like a man.

The Writer: Did you carry on with women on the road?

The Ballplayer: Early on, I did. But I was pretty discreet about that part of my life. I never went out to a bar with the whole team and picked up a woman with everybody watching. That was never my style. I was the Lone Ranger when it came to that kind of business.

The Writer: Then how would you make your connections?

The Ballplayer: A bellboy, a maitre d', a parking lot attendant. I had a whole network of brothers who would hip me on everything — from where to get the best ribs to where to find the foxiest ladies. Sometimes they'd tell me other things, too. Let me tell you, hotel walls have ears. They would tell me who was sleeping with who, and even what guys on the team told nigger jokes in their rooms.

The Writer: Did you ever get burned womanizing?

The Ballplayer: In '62, the same year I had that batting title run with Jimmy Ray Hart, I got hit with a paternity suit. At the time, I was just a kid, twenty years old. The ladies were giving me a lot of attention. There'd been a big write-up about me in the *Pittsburgh Courier*, a black newspaper. It told how much money I'd signed for and all about my big future. So this girl I dated a couple of times comes to me, a black girl, tells me she's pregnant and I'm the father. I don't buy it for a second. She's already got three kids by three different guys. The way I figure it, I'm a long-odds suspect. But first thing, she starts making a lot of noise, and pretty soon the Phillies front office is calling me in for a talk. I told them, don't worry, it's not mine.

The Writer: They believed you?

The Ballplayer: Are you kidding? John Quinn, the Phillies general manager, decides I'm guilty, and pays the lady five thousand dollars to forget about it. Six months later, the baby's born and he's whiter than a fresh-fallen snow in Wampum. But by then it doesn't matter. The Phillies, to their way of thinking, have bailed me out of a jam, and in their eyes I'm beholden to them. A lot of guys would have been, but then a lot of guys aren't Dick Allen.

The Writer: Were paternity suits common?

The Ballplayer: Common with black ballplayers — that's how clubs got their leverage come contract time. In the sixties, it was paternity suits and booze, in the seventies joint and cocaine, now they just say a player has "a problem." Next time you hear a ballplayer referred to that way, check to see if he's white or black. I'll give odds.

The Writer: Come contract time, you always seemed to know exactly what you were doing.

The Ballplayer: I had my own system. At the start of contract negotiations, I would write down on a piece of paper just what I wanted in the deal. Rule one, no standard player's contract. On a separate piece of paper, I would write down the amount of money I wanted. When it was time to talk turkey, I would slide the piece of paper with the money request across the desk. Another Dick Allen rule, never verbalize the amount of money you want. Let the Man do all the talking. After he finished what he had to

say, I would get up and thank him for his time. If he was
going to agree to the money, this is the time he would say
it. If he didn't, I would thank him for his time and leave.
Once the money was agreed upon, I would make *him* sign
a paper that spelled out everything *I* wanted.

The Writer: Wouldn't it be easier to just spell it out in
legal terms?

The Ballplayer: It's easy for an owner or a general
manager to renege on a legal contract. It's much harder
when the terms are spelled out in simple language between
two men.

The Writer: About Al Campanis, the former Dodgers
executive — were you surprised by his comments about
blacks in baseball on network television?

The Ballplayer: This was news? Do you think there was
a black man anywhere in baseball surprised by this? We've
always known the front office was closed to us. They might
as well hang out a sign: NO COLORED. Campanis just let out
what the rest of white baseball wanted to keep secret. The
story's been there all along. But do you think America
wanted to read it? Do you think America wants to hear it
now?

The Writer: You don't think Campanis's remarks will
bring about changes?

The Ballplayer: There'll be talk. We know not to trust
it. We've been hearing that noise all our lives. Ask the
brothers among us who wanted to play quarterback on the
football team and were moved to halfback. Or the black
baseball players who wanted to be pitchers but were shut-
tled to the outfield. Quarterbacks and pitchers are thought
to be the center of the universe in football and baseball — that's why the black athletes are often moved to other

positions. Today, it's business as usual, except now it's out in the open for all to see and it's embarrassing for the guys in business suits.

The Writer: Is there a solution?

The Ballplayer: One — Brotherball. America's prominent black businessmen should get together, people like Berry Gordy of Motown, Bill Cosby, and Julius Erving, and launch an all-black major league franchise. They should locate the team right in the middle of Washington, D.C. — Chocolatetown, USA. They say blacks don't come to baseball games anymore? Watch.

The Writer: An all-black major league franchise?

The Ballplayer: Hey baby! All brothers and sisters. Blacks would run the front office, the coaching staff, accounting, the broadcast team — all of it. Put it out there and let the rest of baseball see our success. With success, the rest of baseball would jump at hiring us all away. Bottom line would win out. That's how to get parity. In the meantime, do you think a few of the brothers might like to play for such a team? Think there might be a few defections?

The Writer: It would certainly bust the myth that blacks aren't suited for front office work.

The Ballplayer: Who do you think ran the Negro Leagues? Blacks owned the teams and ran the teams. It's a nice gesture that major league baseball is beginning to honor Negro League players by inducting them into the Hall of Fame. But if baseball wanted to really honor the Negro Leagues, they would hire black front office people immediately as a tribute to the black men and women who ran the front offices in the Negro Leagues back in the pre–Jackie Robinson days.

The Writer: Who are some of the people you would want to see administer a black franchise?

The Ballplayer: Bob Gibson, Frank Robinson, Mike Schmidt, Bill Robinson, Joe Morgan, Richie Ashburn, Hank Allen, Garry Maddox, Vada Pinson, Tony Taylor, Joe Lonnett, Bill White, Dave Winfield, Chuck Tanner, Lou Brock, Willie Stargell, Henry Aaron, Tim McCarver, Tommy Davis, Joe Torre, Frank Torre, Billy Williams, a kid named Dick Allen. I could go on.

The Writer: Not Reggie Jackson?

The Ballplayer: I love Reggie Jackson, don't get me wrong. But Reggie Jackson is the Don King of baseball. Where were all his strong opinions about blacks in baseball when he was in his prime? Then it was Reggie, Reggie, Reggie. Now that the curtain has come down on the Reggie Jackson career, he's suddenly a man with a lot to say. My question with Reggie has always been the same: Does he love baseball enough to be good for the game?

The Writer: Reggie certainly knows how to get ink.

The Ballplayer: Yes, and it violates the way black players have been taught to play the game. Ever notice that black players don't play to the camera? You never saw Bob Gibson ham it up. Or Henry Aaron. Yet there are certain players that know how to get fan reaction with that extra bit of show biz. It's calculated, too, because they know it'll translate into dollars off the field later. How many times have we seen Pete Rose slide headfirst into a base that he already had stolen? The black player will walk in standing up. Reggie is the one black player who played baseball like it was a prime-time television show.

The Writer: What are some of the subtle aspects of prejudice in baseball?

The Ballplayer: All my career I had people tell me I was a natural hitter. Never once did they take into account how I studied the pitchers, how I analyzed the defense.

Stan Musial and Ted Williams were great students of the game. Henry Aaron and Frank Robinson were naturals. It's patronizing and insulting, and what's worse, people think they're being complimentary when they say it.

The Writer: You don't think the black ballplayer gets enough credit for hard work?

The Ballplayer: No. Never did and never will. The black ballplayer is the innovator in sports. Willie Mays changed the way baseball is played in the outfield with his basket catch. Lou Brock changed the whole art of base running with his quick stutter-step jump off first. These guys didn't just get out of bed and start doing their thing. They worked on their craft as kids, honed it in the minors, and let it rip when they were ready. Innovation is hard work. So is making a thing look easy.

The Writer: Why are the black athletes the innovators?

The Ballplayer: When you grow up poor, you have to improvise your time. You don't get sent to camp, you don't go on vacation, you don't get sent to sports clinics. It's you, the sandlot, the playground, and a lot of hours. So a Willie Mays first learns to catch a fly ball and then he learns how to basket-catch a fly ball. It's his fun. Then he figures out that with his speed he's in better throwing position after a basket catch than he is when he catches in the traditional way. That kind of innovation could never happen in a structured baseball camp.

The Writer: Who are some of your favorite black innovators in sports?

The Ballplayer: Let's take basketball — Connie Hawkins. He was the first dude to come into basketball and start throwing the ball every which way but loose. Wait! He might bounce-pass the base line. No! The Hawk's going around his back to the big man. Hold it, my man! That was a fake! He's taking it to the hoop! Good gracious. Nobody ever saw basketball like that. It damn near scared folks. Connie Hawkins never got the recognition. The guys that came after him were innovators in their own right, too — Pearl Monroe, Julius Erving, Isiah Thomas, Michael Jordan, Magic Johnson.

The Writer: Wilt Chamberlain?

The Ballplayer: Yes, indeed. And Philly-style, too. Here was a man, never appreciated. Nobody loves a giant, especially a black giant. But Wilt was a man who revolutionized basketball. I watched him all through my Philadelphia years. Tremendous strength, and mentally even tougher. This is a man who scored one hundred points in a professional basketball game. A superb athlete. He brought the finger roll into basketball. Yet people thought because he was seven foot two it was easy for him. Wilt never got the credit for revolutionizing the game. Would he have gotten the credit had he been white?

The Writer: Would he?

The Ballplayer: I'll say this. There still hasn't been a white center in basketball like him. Wilt took years of abuse. Guys hanging on him, hacking him on the arms, in the gut, everywhere but the top of his head. On top of that, he had people calling him a freak and asking him how the weather was up there. All he wanted was to do his job. Look at Wilt now. He plays volleyball, he throws discus, he travels around the world. Remember how Bill Walton looked trying to play at the end of his career? He was damn near dead. Not Wilt. They still talk of signing him up to play. Wilt was something, brother.

The Writer: Do you think the black ballplayer and the white ballplayer share a similar work ethic?

The Ballplayer: As a rule, the white and the black ballplayer work equally hard. Difference is, the black ball-player only lets it show when it makes good baseball sense. You remember when Pete Rose would draw a walk, he would take off for first like he just got bit in the ass. You watch Vince Coleman and you'll see he takes his time getting to first on a walk. He puts his energy on reserve for when he needs it.

The Writer: Speaking of speed, you were never given enough credit for your base running skills.

The Ballplayer: Base running is an art and a skill. Not base stealing — base *running*. If I'm on second, one ball on the batter, I'm going to try to get a big lead to distract the pitcher. My job is to help get ball two. Now the pitcher's got to throw a strike. Batter knows that, I know that. He's in a position to get good wood on the ball. He gets a single, I score. That's good base running.

The Writer: If you were making up your all-time baseball team, who would it include?

The Ballplayer: Here's your Dick Allen lineup card:

> Jackie Robinson, second base
> Ernie Banks, shortstop
> Willie Mays, center field
> Henry Aaron, right field
> Cool Papa Bell, left field
> Mike Schmidt, third base
> Willie Stargell, first base
> Josh Gibson, catcher

The Writer: Mike Schmidt might feel a little lonely.

The Ballplayer: Black ballplayers know what it feels like to be lonely. Mike Schmidt is the baddest white boy I've ever seen play the game. Period.

The Writer: Your pitching staff?

The Ballplayer: Give me Satchel Paige, Bob Gibson, Sandy Koufax, and Bob Veale.

The Writer: How about your manager?

The Ballplayer: Danny Murtaugh, the old Pirates skipper. Murtaugh was absolutely color-blind. If nine black guys were the best players on the team, nine black guys would be in the starting lineup. He never took a black or white head count. I grew up watching Murtaugh pilot the Pirates. He was a smart baseball man, and tough as horsehide.

The Writer: Has money screwed up baseball?

The Ballplayer: It's not the money itself; it's the way the players relate to the money. I made very good money playing major league baseball. But I never let the money get in the way. The Phillies used to bring my paycheck down to me in the clubhouse because I'd forget to pick it up. My first priority was winning the damn games. Now the players spend their off-hours deciding whether to invest their money in mutual funds or racquetball courts. The game itself becomes an afterthought.

The Writer: What was the hardest aspect of baseball life off the field?

The Ballplayer: Sportswriters. Most ballplayers think of sportswriters as vermin — and some are just that. Many of them are frustrated jocks. The sportswriting life is completely alien to the life of a professional athlete. Ballplayers can't understand why a person would want to make his living hanging out at ballparks with notebooks and typewriters. I know I can't.

The Writer: Why did you have such a hard time with sportswriters?

The Ballplayer: I didn't play by their rules. Sportswriters expect you to cooperate with them just because they have the final say. They can write what they want, true or not, and you have no say in how the story reads in the paper the next day. I decided early on that that wouldn't go with me.

The Writer: You wouldn't talk to them?

The Ballplayer: Sometimes I would; sometimes I wouldn't. Those guys would come around and mess up my concentration with all their questions. So I just did the same to them. If I was in the mood, I would sit down and answer whatever they asked me. The next day, I would tell the same guy to get out of my face. It threw them off their stride. They resented the lack of control — and they'd get back at me in print.

The Writer: Weren't they just trying to do their jobs?

The Ballplayer: Maybe, but poorly. After a while, I knew exactly where each guy was coming from. Dick Young, the late New York columnist, was out to make me look like a shiftless black ballplayer because that's what he thought of all black ballplayers. Stan Hochman, a writer for the *Philadelphia Daily News*, would always lead with the hard-ass question because he thought he had to be the macho guy, the tough-guy writer. Bob Verdi, the Chicago writer, would always bring up old dirt and throw it into every column he wrote about me. Larry Merchant, when he was a sportswriter, was always on the hustle — he had his eye on bigger things, and Dick Allen was one way to help him get there. After a while you get on to these guys. It doesn't take a brain surgeon to figure out their deal.

The Writer: Were there sportswriters you liked?

The Ballplayer: There was one cat — Ray Kelly. He used to write for the old *Philadelphia Bulletin*. He had an approach I could relate to. He'd wait for a quiet moment, then he'd come over to me and ask me to explain whatever happened to be going on at the time. He didn't pretend that he was performing some great service to mankind. We'd go out and get a beer and talk about things calmly, man to man. Another guy I liked, Sandy Padwe.

The Writer: In retrospect, do you wish you had been more open with writers?

The Ballplayer: It just wasn't possible. When I explain things, I like to give the whole picture. Writers don't have the patience for that kind of introspection. They want quick-hit answers to fit into their columns for the next day's paper.

The Writer: Things might have been different had you chosen to tell your side of the Frank Thomas story.

The Ballplayer: Maybe. But I would have had to explain too much background. I would have had to explain how Thomas used to always pick on Wes Covington, one of our teammates. I liked Wes, but he was a lot different than me. He talked all the time. I mean, all the time. Covington's nickname was "the Kingfish." For Thomas, that meant open season. He would say to Covington, "Here, boy, shine my shoes." Or "The sun's blazing out there today, Wes. You gonna work on your tan?" Covington used to take that, but it would burn my ass.

The Writer: You didn't want to hurt Covington?

The Ballplayer: Exactly. I remember turning to Callison in the clubhouse and telling him that if Thomas begins directing that garbage at me — duck! When Thomas said a couple of things to me, I walked over to him and said, "Frank, I'm not like Wes. I don't appreciate that kind of thing. It don't go with me."

The Writer: Do you wish you had done anything differently in the Thomas affair?

The Ballplayer: I would have hit him harder. He never would have had the chance to hit me with a bat.

The Writer: Besides sportswriters, were there other distractions that threw you off your game?

The Ballplayer: There was a certain kind of fan, and I still get it sometimes, who wants to have a personal debate with you. They'll come up to you anywhere and tell you their opinion of this guy or that guy, or how they think you should have handled a certain situation on the field. All they really want to do is hear themselves talk. They'll ask you a question, and before you can answer it, they're trying to answer it for you. With a guy like that, I always ask him what he does for a living. If he's a dentist, I start telling him all I know about teeth. That usually does the trick. Nobody likes an uninformed opinion.

•7•

Shuffled

In the autumn of 1969, four full seasons after the Ballplayer
first asked to be traded, Bob Carpenter, the reluctant but
controversy-weary Phillies owner, finally yielded to Allen's
demand. The trade: Allen, Cookie Rojas, and Jerry Johnson to the Cardinals for Curt Flood, Tim McCarver, Joe
Hoerner, and Byron Browne. In essence, Allen for Flood.
The Phillies seemed pleased with the deal: In Flood they
would get a thirty-one-year-old outfielder with a .293 lifetime batting average. One glitch. Flood refused to go to
Philadelphia. Instead, he announced he was challenging baseball's reserve clause.

To Allen, Flood's decision to fight for free agency was
just one more strange and ironic twist in his own major
league career. "There I was," the Ballplayer explains, "off
to St. Louis, free as a cardinal, determined to be Mr. Low
Profile Man. Next thing I know, here comes Curtis, saying
he ain't going nowhere. Now there's lots of controversy,
lots of headlines, and who's right in the thick of it? Richard
Anthony Allen.

What's more, the Ballplayer felt a deep kinship with
Flood's refusal to go along with the trade. By 1969, Allen

was no longer asking the Phillies to trade him; he was demanding it. The difference was that while Flood wanted control over where he was being sent to ply his trade, the Ballplayer had but a single priority: getting out of Philadelphia. The way Allen saw it then, and the way he continues to see it today, free agency is made complicated not by the ballplayers but by a lack of vision on the part of baseball owners.

"The freer you make baseball in every respect," the Ballplayer explains, "the better the game's going to be. We saw that with Jackie Robinson. Jackie liberated the game. He was free. Free to steal home. Free to turn a single into a double. Free to play his game with a sense of danger and urgency. That same sense of freedom should apply to free agency. If baseball owners would concentrate on making their franchises exciting and happy places, instead of work camps where guys punch in and out, ballplayers would *fight* to stay. Loyalty would only make the game better. Today's owners don't build ball teams, only ballclubs. The day some owner wakes up and decides that giving ballplayers their freedom is the secret to putting together a happy and winning ball team, baseball will have a serious dynasty on their hands."

That spring of '69, while Flood waited for the courts to decide his fate, Allen stayed home in Philadelphia, a hold-out, two weeks of Cardinals spring training already gone. The Cards' offer: $85,000; Allen's counter: $150,000. Cardinals owner Gussie Busch, incensed at the changing mores of baseball and perplexed that his ballplayers suddenly, inexplicably, wanted control of their own destinies, lashed out to the press at spring training camp: "I can't understand Rich Allen. I can't understand Curt Flood. We have to take a stand for the good of baseball."

Busch then slapped Allen with an ultimatum: sign or get signed. He gave the Ballplayer twenty-four hours to decide, invoking paragraph 10 of the reserve clause. Paragraph 10 stated that a team had the right to force a player to report at any salary it wanted to write into a contract as long as that figure was not less than 80 percent of the previous season's contract. In citing paragraph 10, the wealthy St. Louis beer baron employed the same type of reserve clause restrictions that had sent Flood into the courts.

Twenty-four hours later, to the surprise of the baseball world, Allen signed with the Cardinals for $85,000.

"Why? One, I wanted to play baseball," says Allen. "I love the game. The Philly years had made me feel like a baseball outlaw. I had built a tough exterior to protect myself. So much had happened — Frank Thomas, Gene Mauch, the hand injury, the fans, the sportswriters — and see, inside me, all that time, all I really wanted to do was play the game. Have some fun, win some ballgames. Being traded to St. Louis gave me hope that maybe I could find the passion again.

"Two, I don't sign, baseball owners use me to discredit free agency. They use Dick Allen as an example of a player who stirs controversy for controversy's sake. Not true, never true, but sounds true. Fits in with the Richie Allen headlines. Using Dick Allen, they could accomplish two things: distract from the principles behind Flood's fight for freedom and kick my ass out of baseball for good. But Dick Allen doesn't get used. I signed their paper. First and last time I laid down at the negotiating table. I had to consider the higher plane."

That spring of 1970, for the first time since '64, *Rich* Allen (as he was inexplicably dubbed by the St. Louis press) found himself reporting to a team with genuine marquee value and bona fide pennant hopes. The Cardinal pitching staff was headed by Bob Gibson, the most feared pitcher in baseball, and Steve Carlton, a 17-game winner in '69 and an emerging superstar. The Cardinal lineup included ballplayers like Joe Torre, Lou Brock, Mike Shannon, Jose Cardenal, and Ted Simmons, experienced and respected veterans all.

It was a Cardinals club that had snagged pennants in '67 and '68, before slipping back to fourth in '69. By the spring of 1970, Cardinals owner Gussie Busch was determined to bring his franchise back to its previous winning ways. But while the Allen trade, on paper, seemed to solidify Cardinals pennant hopes, some St. Louis sportswriters wondered in print whether the Ballplayer's mercurial personality would clash with the big Cardinal names already in the St. Louis clubhouse.

Hardly the case. "In terms of personality, the Cardinals were my kind of team," recalls the Ballplayer. "Guys that could gig. Any concern I had about my new teammates vanished when I arrived in St. Petersburg for spring training. I walked into the clubhouse and found a magazine article taped to my locker. It was headlined THE FIVE MOST OVER-RATED PLAYERS IN BASEBALL. I was one of the five. So was Joe Torre, my new teammate. The other three were Ken Harrelson, Sam McDowell, and Joe Pepitone. Someone had scribbled: 'Two out of five ain't bad.' I looked around the clubhouse and saw Bob Gibson giggling in the corner. 'Welcome to the Cardinals,' Gibbie yelled at me. I would have laughed, but I was too busy trying to figure out why Carl Yastrzemski wasn't on the list."

With Gibson clearly established as the main man in the Cardinals clubhouse, the Ballplayer felt assured that, unlike the case in Philadelphia, there would be little in the way of racial tension on or off the field. Adding to Allen's sense of security was the fact that in 1970 the Cardinals manager was Red Schoendienst, known affectionately by everyone in baseball as the "Old Redhead." Unlike Gene Mauch, Schoendienst as a manager was among the most passive — and successful — in baseball. Schoendienst had taken the Cardinals from sixth place in '66 to a world championship in '67.

The Ballplayer still remembers how the Cardinal manager greeted his arrival: "First time he saw me, Red stuck out his hand and said, 'Rich, I've seen it all. I played nineteen years in the bigs, I've been spiked, I've been beaned, I've had to deal with Bob Gibson in my clubhouse, I've licked tuberculosis, for God's sake. There's nothing left for me to prove. The reporters are already asking me how I'm going to handle Rich Allen. I told them, and now I'm telling you, I ain't handling anybody. Put your uniform on and have fun. You won't get any heat from me.'

"I knew right away that I was going to like Red better than Mauch. Red had played the game. He was a ballplayer first. Not a cup-of-coffee major leaguer like Mauch, but big time. Hit .300 or better seven times, played a slick second base. He didn't need to show ballplayers who was boss. He'd been there. Ballplayers know when their manager played in the Show."

Anxious to recast his image, Allen took literally his new manager's mandate to have fun and even began giving playful interviews to the press. When he arrived in St. Louis following spring training and was asked what he thought of the new artificial surface in Busch Stadium, the Ballplayer quipped, "If horses won't eat it, I don't want to play on it."

Allen's quote was picked up around the country and was even used as a parting shot on an NBC national newscast. This was the kind of baseball fun Allen had always dreamed about — and what's more, the people of St. Louis seemed to actually enjoy their new slugger's lighthearted irreverence.

Allen retains warm feelings about St. Louis to this day: "St. Louis baseball is All-American style. Not like Philly. Not like New York. Not like anywhere else. In St. Louis, the fans care about the game. In other cities, especially New York and Philly, it's all about personalities. Here, they talked strategy — the hit-and-run, the squeeze play, the defensive alignment. It was great therapy for me. These fans didn't care about off-the-field controversies. Before I got to St. Louis Roger Maris and Orlando Cepeda had played for the Cardinals, two guys who had been roughed up by fans pretty badly in other cities. But both Maris and Cepeda had found homes in St. Louis. I was hopeful they would appreciate my game and let me play it on my own terms."

Buoyed by his new surroundings, the Ballplayer showed his appreciation in classic Dick Allen style. In his first two games as a Cardinal he went 5 for 10, including a homer and three doubles, leading the Cardinals to a two-game opening sweep in Montreal against the Expos and their new manager — Gene Mauch. Prior to the Ballplayer's smashing debut as a Cardinal, Mauch had told the St. Louis writers: "Allen's a great athlete and his teammates and the St. Louis fans will love him. He's a good team man. You won't see many 0s, 1s and 2s next to the Cardinals' name this year because number 15 will take care of that."

By the time the team arrived in St. Louis to begin the first home stand of the season, Rich Allen — unlike the

Richie Allen who had played in Philadelphia — had become an instant folk hero. When veteran Cardinals broadcaster Jack Buck announced the Ballplayer's name as he stepped to the plate as a Redbird for the first time at Busch Stadium, the St. Louis faithful — 50,000 strong — greeted their new slugger with a ninety-second standing ovation.

There are times when Allen can still hear the roar. "I didn't know how to react. I'd been playing in anger with the boos for so long. I kept stepping in and out of the batter's box. I tipped my hat once, but the cheers kept coming. I stepped out again and tipped my hat again. I was trying to keep my composure, but tears kept filling my eyes. I was twenty-eight years old — and an old twenty-eight at that. All those angry seasons in Philadelphia had taken their toll, but the cheers made me feel like a teenager. Afterward one of the Cardinals writers told me that it was the most sustained ovation he'd ever heard in St. Louis. 'You'd have thought Musial had come out of retirement' is the way he put it."

By mid-May, the Ballplayer had hit 11 home runs and was off to the finest start of his career.

"Instead of hitting the ball in anger and muscling the ball out of the park, like I had in Philly for five seasons, I was now swinging in freedom. I was relaxed at the plate, maybe for the first time in my professional career. The result was that I could stay with breaking pitches longer. I discovered that playing loose and happy baseball gave me more options. I could still go long ball, but now I could also stay with a pitch longer and hit a flare down the line instead — and I could make the decision to do either in a microsecond with a downward flick of my wrists. I was playing Wampum ball."

*   *   *

That same month of May 1970, the Ballplayer returned to Philadelphia and Connie Mack Stadium for the first time since leaving the Phillies organization. With the Phillies he had been a target; now, as a Cardinal, he was the enemy. It was a Richie Allen homecoming.

"Twelve thousand Philadelphia fans came out for the first game of that Cardinals-Phillies series," Allen recalls. "Doesn't sound like much, but it was twice the turnout for any Phillies game to that point. That crowd made more noise than any baseball crowd I've heard before or since. The Connie Mack Stadium crazies were out, too. Before the game, Gibson came over to me on the bench and told me to take a look behind the dugout. I stuck my head out and saw this guy kneeling on the dugout roof, wearing a Phillies hat sideways on his head. When he saw me, he said, 'What's happenin', lushhead?' I knew I was home."

On his first trip to the plate in that opening game of the series, the Ballplayer grounded into a double play. The Philadelphia fans bellowed their approval. When Allen came to the plate in the ninth inning, the Phillies were leading, 3–0.

First pitch, high fastball. "Hel-lo Philadelphia! I got all of it. It started out as a low line drive but went airborne just past the shortstop's head and crashed against an empty seat in left field. When I reached home plate, I instinctively raised my fist in the air. Afterward, it was reported I did it for spite or to make a racial statement of some kind. Not true. It was the ninth inning. I wanted to win. That's all.

"Unfortunately, we didn't rally. My home run got us two, but it ended three to two, Phils. Afterward, the Philadelphia sportswriters crowded around my locker in the visitors' clubhouse. Did I feel vindicated? Was I sticking it to the Philadelphia fans? *Say what?* I knew then that some things would never change. For six years I'd been telling these same Philadelphia sportswriters that Dick Allen only cared about one thing, winning baseball games. But they preferred the Rich Allen soap opera over the game itself. I couldn't wait to get back to St. Louis."

Despite Allen's potent bat, the Cardinals had gotten off to a ragged start in 1970. One reason was the loss of Mike Shannon, the starting third baseman. Shannon had been sidelined with a mysterious kidney ailment that took him out of the lineup early. The Shannon injury forced Schoendienst to juggle his lineup card frequently; Allen was affected most directly, being moved from first base, where he had started the season, back to third base, a position he thought he had left behind in Philadelphia. Once again, the Ballplayer was without a position to call his own.

"In my five years with the Phillies, I played left field, third base, a couple of games at shortstop, and, in '69, just before coming to St. Louis, 117 games at first base. I had come to consider myself a first baseman. But being shifted from one corner of the diamond to the other and back again was *worse* than being back at third. I went to Red and told him I wanted to play first. What does Red do? He tosses me the lineup card. 'Here you go, Rich,' he says. 'Pencil yourself in.' Then he says, 'While you're at it, fill in the rest of the lineup. Maybe you'll have better luck.' I had to admit, I liked Red's style."

Despite the horrendous start, by August the team had managed to go from last place to fourth place, just nine and a half games out with two months to go. But instead of surging forward, the '70 Cardinals seemed content to settle for respectability.

The attitude of some of his Cardinals teammates in 1970 still rankles the Ballplayer: "We had a shot at the flag going into August. But a lot of the guys on the team didn't have the faith. I remember going around the clubhouse doing a Gene Mauch, trying to fire everybody up. I kept telling the new guys that it was the Cardinals — this *very* club — who came up on the Phillies to rip off that pennant in '64. Brock and Gibson were with the Cards in '64, so they knew, and I sure knew. But you've got to witness one to get the faith."

Then in the second week of August, disaster. Legging out a two-base hit, the Ballplayer tore a hamstring sliding into second. At the time of the injury, Allen had already hit 33 home runs and driven in 100. He had recently been voted by the fans as the National League's starting All-Star first baseman over Willie McCovey, Ernie Banks, and Orlando Cepeda. Now, suddenly, the Ballplayer's season of rebirth was over.

"I was desolate," he recalls. "St. Louis had been good to me. It had been a good season. Off the field, I was like a choir boy. No drink, no horses, no messing around. I had sold two of my three horses. That left me just one, which I had left back in Philadelphia with Barbara. I'd lived the whole season in a hotel room near the St. Louis airport. When the team was home, my son Dickie would fly in from Philadelphia and stay with me. Every night we'd order ribs and chicken and eat in the room. Every night, same routine. I wanted no distractions, no chance of missing a flight. I wanted 1970 to be the year that Dick Allen proved he could play baseball and stay out of headlines."

Immediately following the injury the Ballplayer left the

club and returned to Philadelphia. The Cardinals front office, upset by Allen's departure, tried to order the Ballplayer back to St. Louis for periodic examinations by the team's doctor. But Allen stayed away. And the headlines returned.

"I wasn't going to get well sitting in a St. Louis hotel room," he explains. "Injuries are both physical and psychological; ballplayers know that better than anybody. When I put my hand through that headlight, I was told I was finished. But my hand healed. It healed because I drove from Philadelphia to California, by myself, which gave me the time and space to heal psychologically. Healing physically is the easy part. I wasn't going to get better being penned up in a St. Louis hotel room. Not Dick Allen style."

Allen would return to the St. Louis Cardinals for one more appearance late that season. The Ballplayer always did have a flair for the stage. Recalls Allen: "It was my last chance to play in Connie Mack Stadium. The Phillies had already announced they would be playing the '71 season in a new stadium. It was an event I knew I'd have to make. I called Red from my house in Philadelphia and told him I wanted to play. He was against it. I begged him. It was personal, I told him."

Only four thousand people came out to Connie Mack Stadium that September night for what was otherwise a meaningless game between the Cardinals and the Phillies. For the Ballplayer, however, crowd or no, it was a night of high emotion. "I didn't belong on the field," he recalls quietly. "My leg was throbbing. I had downed a couple of drinks to numb the pain. I had a lot of mixed emotions. In the eighth inning I came to the plate for what I knew would be my last time in Connie Mack Stadium. Rick Wise was on the mound. I had played with Rick the season before. Good heat. I knew to wait. Second pitch, I sent a fastball into the left-field seats. It was my ninetieth home run in Connie Mack Stadium — and my last.

"As I rounded the bases, I took one last look around. I looked up at the press box, where so many negative stories had been written about me. I looked up at the Cadillac and Coke signs, where I had hit so many home runs for my first major league team, the Philadelphia Phillies. I looked into the stands, where they had called me every name known to man. I touched home plate and kept running. When I got to the clubhouse, I showered and left before the writers got there. I had nothing to say. I wanted to let that home run stand on its own as Dick Allen's goodbye to that house of gloom."

The Cardinals finished 1970 in fourth place. Though the St. Louis front office was disappointed, there seemed no way that Allen could be blamed — not with 34 home runs and 101 RBIs in 122 games played. "I was disappointed with our finish in the standings, but I was looking forward to the '71 season," Allen recalls. "I was getting to like St. Louis, to feel comfortable. Then, a couple of weeks after the season, I got a call from Bing Devine, the Cardinals general manager. 'Rich,' he said, 'we're sending you to the Dodgers.' That's all he said. No explanation. No good luck. No thanks."

A *St. Louis Globe-Democrat* story published the day after the trade, headlined CARDS PEDDLE ALLEN TO HELP TEAM MORALE, claimed that Schoendienst had employed one set of rules for twenty-four Cardinals and a different set of rules for Rich Allen. "You know why that was written?" says the Ballplayer. "Because I gave an in-depth interview to a writer from a competing paper. True. And this cat got his back up. The writer I *gave* the interview to reported that Rich Allen's morale was down — which it was — but then he explained it. I was down because I wanted a pennant and we hadn't even come close. I tasted it in '64. I couldn't get the thought of winning one out of my head. I thought winning was the idea. But that wasn't the story people wanted to read. The other story is a better seller. Dick Allen being a screw-off sells more newspapers."

In the weeks following, Allen thought about giving up baseball. "I'd done everything expected of me. I only went to the racetrack twice all year. I worked hard — along with Torre, Brock, and Gibson — to keep team morale high. I kicked butt out on the diamond. I brought people into the park. We drew a million and a half fans. That's box office. I did everything except sell beer. Clearly, I'd been labeled, blackballed. No amount of staying out of trouble was going to change what the baseball establishment thought of me. I felt like a con on indefinite parole. The people of St. Louis knew there'd been an injustice. The baseball fans in St. Louis damn near lynched Gussie Busch for that trade. When the Cardinals told me I'd been traded, I asked what they got in return. They told me Ted Sizemore and a catcher named Bob Stinson. No disrespect intended, but Sizemore and Stinson for a Dick Allen? I'd like to know what the guys in the St. Louis front office were smoking the night that deal went down."

Los Angeles, summer '87

We're sitting, writer and Ballplayer, at a picnic table near the Ballplayer's North Hollywood apartment, sipping Heinekens. Collaboration, California style.

On this day, under God's golden sunshine, the Ballplayer shows no sign of the boredom he sometimes exhibits when the subject is Dick Allen's life in baseball. The Ballplayer prefers to speak about baseball spontaneously, and then only in riffs; linear thinking, particularly when it pertains to his own past performances, is anathema to Allen. To the Ballplayer, baseball is performance art; to pick that performance apart, to analyze and study it, to critique it, particularly in retrospect, is to dismiss the romantic and ironic shadings that are the game itself.

But on this sunny California afternoon we have come with a specific agenda: 1971, the Ballplayer's sole season with the Los Angeles Dodgers. We begin with the weather. It is one of the reasons Allen lives in California much of the year.

"The sun out here chills people out. You can also be anonymous here. Everybody's too busy doing things outside to notice. And there's a lot of natural beauty here. When I played with the Dodgers I would get up at dawn and go down to the beach to bat pebbles into the ocean. I had a broomstick that I kept in the trunk of my car. That was batting practice. I could hear myself think and find my swing. No writers. No autographs. I could hit stones high into the sky, then watch them fall far into the ocean with the sun coming up in my face. When I played here, I was very close to myself, and by getting close to myself, I could get close to God."

In '71 the Ballplayer found himself playing for his third team in as many years. Though the controversies had abated, the label persisted. Many baseball insiders expressed surprise that the Dodger organization was willing to payroll a Dick Allen, who didn't exactly fit the Dodger image.

The Ballplayer remembers being a bit surprised himself. "When the Phillies agreed to trade me after the '69 season the Dodgers kept coming up in the newspapers as a possibility. They needed a big stick in the lineup. But Al Campanis, the Dodger general manager, kept telling writers that he wanted my bat — but not my personality. He said I would be a travesty to the Dodger spirit. Hurt my feelings, because I always thought I had a pretty good personality."

I suggest that perhaps the Dodger organization may have been influenced by those 34 home runs for St. Louis in 1970.

"In '70 the Dodgers had hit only ninety homers all season. They *needed* Dick Allen power. Then again, maybe Mr. Campanis figured a little personality might actually help the Dodgers. Remember, Walter Alston was the manager of the Dodgers. Compared to Walt, I did have a strong personality. Compared to Walt, everybody did."

The Ballplayer signed with the Dodgers for $100,000, his first six-figure contract, and even reported to spring training early, just to demonstrate his enthusiasm.

"Becoming a Dodger was a dream right out of imaginary baseball. I was in my own Dodgers lineup. I got goose bumps putting on the Jackie Robinson blue and white threads. I was so anxious to please that I ran into a palm tree in the outfield shagging fly balls the first week of spring training at Vero Beach. I shouldn't have been surprised. Spring training and I never did see eye to eye. One time I take it serious and I knock myself out."

The Ballplayer recalls his first impression of baseball, Dodger style.

"On the surface, Alston was a lot like Schoendienst. Both were low-key. Difference was, Alston's coaches — his lieutenants — would do all the day-to-day things. Then they'd report back to him. That was the Dodger way, organization. Still is. Alston used to stand at the edge of the dugout during games and toss pebbles. One after another. Never changing expression. Guys used to say that you could set Walt's butt on fire and he'd still stand there, tossing pebbles. He'd been tossing pebbles for seventeen years when I got there in '71."

Walter Alston's 1971 Dodgers were a fairly pedestrian lot by the Ballplayer's imaginary baseball standards.

"We did have some good ballplayers — Wes Parker, Steve Garvey, Willie Davis, Bobby Valentine. Gritty guys. Al Downing won twenty for us that year. But did we have a Koufax? A Drysdale? A Duke Snider? A Jackie Robinson? No, baby. But we did have a kid named Allen. The problem was all that Dodger Blue jive. Not Dick Allen style. The organization tries to get you to believe that being a Dodger is all you've ever needed in this world. They want you to feel blessed. It's one way they keep their players in tow. A lot of guys fall for it.

"The Dodger organization also emphasizes contact with the fans. They put a lot of pressure on players to sign autographs and have their picture taken. They want you to visit with celebs in the clubhouse before games. Have a laugh with Don Rickles. Eat spaghetti with Sinatra. I kept telling these guys, un-uh, no, baby, I'm here to play ball, that other stuff is jive. It distracts from the team's mission to win ballgames. Like I say, I was proud to be a Dodger because of Jackie Robinson. That was where it ended."

The Los Angeles baseball fan was also an alien phenomenon, according to the Ballplayer.

"After I'd hit a home run in Dodger Stadium, I'd look up into the stands and everybody would be on their feet applauding. Politely. They did everything except say 'bravo.' It was baseball as theater. I used to fantasize what Dodger Stadium would be like filled with New York and Philadelphia baseball fans. Imagine, just once, a Dodger Stadium overflowing with East Coast bad asses. No laid-back California folks. I'd be willing to finance such an experiment."

In 1971 the Dodgers finished only two games out of first place.

"We should have won it. Problem was, we allowed ourselves to be intimidated by the Giants — McCovey, Bonds, Mays, that gang. The Giants may have had more talent, but still no reason to roll over. We beat ourselves with all that LA show biz. We had one guy on the team playing the banjo, one guy trying to be a comic, another guy who showed up on soap operas, stupid stuff. Guys began to believe the Dodger propaganda that baseball was show business. Instead of gigging, guys were watching the board to see what the Giants were doing. You can't win pennants unless you play aggressive baseball. We had some crybabies."

I bring up the name of Maury Wills.

"You heard it, too? I have respect for every guy who has pulled on a big league uniform. But true is true, and Maury Wills was a morale breaker. He was out to grab as many stolen bases as he could. That's where he found his glory. The stolen base thing got to his head. For him, it was bigger than winning. If he didn't swipe a couple of bases over the course of a series, he'd begin to sulk. It would affect the whole team. In Dick Allen's book, Maury Wills was a great base stealer, one of the best of all time, but not a smart base runner."

The '71 season ended with the Ballplayer compiling a .295 average and hitting only 23 home runs.

"Off my game all season. Jackie Robinson was long gone. The Dodgers only wanted me for a quick fix. After the '71 season, they told me I was traded to the White Sox for Tommy John. I couldn't get myself to even care. The fix was in. Dick Allen was a guy to use for one year and then trade off. I was getting the quick shuffle. I was only in my eighth season of baseball, but that's what baseball had become for me — a fast shuffle to oblivion."

•8•

MVP

Summertime '87. I find Chuck Tanner, the manager of the Atlanta Braves, standing between the Braves dugout and home plate. His arms are folded across his chest and his eyes are fixed on the batting cage. It is a warm southern kind of summer Sunday morning, and the Braves are taking their pregame cuts. It is Tanner's eighteenth season as a baseball manager and one of his most trying: His Braves are buried in the basement.

But even when under siege, as he is at this particular juncture in his long and winding baseball career, Chuck Tanner has the gentle look of a favorite uncle, the kind of guy who likes nothing better than a good pitching duel and a cold bottle of Ballantine on a muggy Sunday afternoon. Tanner is from New Castle, Pennsylvania, just twenty miles up the road from Wampum, Pennsylvania, mill country. But despite his many years in the big leagues Tanner hasn't lost his western Pennsylvania blue-collar values. He likes to call himself a baseball workingman.

At age fifty-eight, Tanner has a nicely browned face from his many summers in the sun; his eyes still dance at the sound of good wood on a baseball, and he still claps his hands like he means it when his team needs a rally. On this day, as each of his players leaves the batting cage, Tanner acknowledges their efforts with a friendly whap on the rump, deserved or not. In baseball circles, Chuck Tanner is known as a ballplayer's manager. Willie Stargell, an Atlanta Braves coach who helped win a World Series for Tanner and the Pittsburgh Pirates in 1979, sets me straight about the way ballplayers feel about his boss: "You don't like playing for Chuck," he says, "you don't like playing the game."

I interrupt Tanner's batting cage reverie to tell him that I've come to Atlanta to talk to him about Dick Allen, a former player of his back in 1972 — the season Tanner, then skipper of the Chicago White Sox, was named the American League's Manager of the Year and Allen the league's Most Valuable Player.

That '72 season, the Chicago White Sox (a team of "has beens and also rans," according to one preseason Chicago scribe) finished just five and a half games behind the talent-laden Oakland A's in the American League West. On paper the Sox appeared a second-division team in the preseason. And the postseason numbers did little to alter that perception; witness Chuck Tanner's opening day lineup card and his team's subsequent batting averages:

> Walt Williams, rf: .249
> Mike Andrews, 2b: .220
> Dick Allen, 1b: .308
> Bill Melton, 3b: .245
> Carlos May, lf: .308
> Rick Reichardt, cf: .251
> Ed Herrmann, c: .249
> Luis Alvarado, ss: .213

But despite such collective anemic hitting (Bill Melton, the Sox — and league — leader in '71 with 33 home runs, was sidelined for the season in June '72 with a herniated disc), the White Sox lost just five more games than the division-winning Oakland A's in '72, a team with a star-studded marquee that included Catfish Hunter, Vida Blue, Sal Bando, Reggie Jackson, Joe Rudi, Gene Tenace, and Bert Campaneris.

When I tell Tanner of my mission, he listens intently but doesn't say anything; instead he leads me by the arm down to the far end of the Braves dugout, away from his ballplayers. When we sit down, he pulls my arm again, hard this time, and leans his face into mine. "In all my years of baseball," Chuck Tanner tells me in a conspiratorial whisper, "I have never seen a season to compare to the one Dick Allen had in 1972. I mean, not even close. It wasn't that he did it all, which he did, it was the *way* he did it. He was on a rampage, a man on a mission. He could do anything he wanted. Dick Allen picked the White Sox up on his back and carried them all season. It was a powerful thing to watch."

I had heard this exact sentiment before, almost word for word, from Roland Hemond, the general manager of the White Sox in '72. When I had asked Hemond about Allen, his memories of '72 gushed out happily: "Allen? He could do anything. One time, I won't ever forget this, [Sox broadcaster] Harry Caray was calling the game from the bleachers in deep center field. Dick couldn't stand Harry. Harry was always shooting off his mouth. So one day Harry's out there, and Dick comes to the plate, and he slams a ball deep, and it's one of those classic Allen shots — it starts low, just clearing second base, and then it begins to go, and go, and go, and all of a sudden it's coming right at Harry, and you can see what's going to happen — everybody around Harry jumps up, and the beer spills everywhere, most of it right on Harry. I don't think Harry believed that the ball could actually reach him. Dick just circled the bases with that mischievous smile of his."

Hemond's got another favorite:

"A doubleheader in early June in '72. We're playing the Yankees. Dick had delivered with a couple of hits in the first game, and Chuck had decided to rest him in the second game. The South Side crowd was on Chuck to put Dick in from the first inning. But Dick sits. Comes the ninth inning. Two on, one out, we're down, 4–2. Sparky Lyle on the mound. It was the season of his life. Nobody could touch him. Now here comes Dick out of the dugout to pinch hit. The crowd was delirious. We all knew what was going to happen. Sure enough, Dick catches a Lyle pitch and rockets it into the left-field upper deck. We win, 5–4. That home run was a high point in White Sox baseball history. I still remember seeing Lyle walk off the mound the moment that ball was hit and then seeing Dick put his fist up in the air as he was rounding first. It was like that around the park all summer. Chicago was the place things happened in baseball that season."

At this point it is worth noting that there are students of the Dick Allen saga — the Philadelphia contingent particularly — who credit Chuck Tanner (and, to a lesser degree, Roland Hemond) with providing the proper comfort level for Allen to do his thing that remarkable season. And it was truly remarkable: in 1972, his first year in the American League, Allen batted .308, hit 37 home runs, scored 90 runs, drove in 113, walked 99 times, stole 19 bases (in 22 attempts), and finished just a fraction of a point behind John Mayberry, the league leader in fielding percentage, at first base.

The relationship between manager (Tanner) and ballplayer (Allen) in 1972 was baseball symbiosis at its finest, the theory goes — both men from neighboring mill towns in western Pennsylvania, both having shared boyhood sandlots. Allen and Tanner knew, liked, and respected each other before the fame and the complexities of big league life; thus their mutual respect was established early.

Fifteen baseball seasons after Chicago '72, I try this theory out on Tanner in the Braves dugout.

"Sure, I knew the Allen family well. I played basketball against one of Dick's brothers in high school. I knew Mrs. Allen, a wonderful woman, a tough woman, raising all those boys by herself. Back home everybody knew about Mrs. Allen and her boys. It was an athletically gifted family, and word goes 'round up there when one family produces so many great athletes. Of course Dick was the Allen boy everybody heard all the big stories about. You'd hear stories about the way he could jam a basketball and hit a ball six hundred feet. But what I knew about Dick from having grown up nearby — and, see, this is what the other people in baseball didn't know — was how much Dick Allen liked to win. It was all he cared about.

"People — the writers, mostly — assumed I was nervous about having Dick come to the Sox, and in reality, I felt just the opposite. I couldn't wait. His reputation, the part about being tough to get along with, was just nonsense, the way I looked at it. When I got the word that Dick was coming over to the Sox, I paid a visit to Wampum and spent some time with Dick and his mom. We sat at the kitchen table for hours and talked about life around Wampum and New Castle, just like the three locals we are.

"Dick was all business right from the start. But I discovered some things about Dick that I didn't know. For one, he had an incredible mind for baseball. He thought like a manager. He saw the whole field. He'd come into the dugout from first base between innings and stand right next to me. He'd say, 'Homey' — that was his personal nickname for me — 'I think next inning we ought to shade the outfield to left when so-and-so comes up.' That's what Dick Allen's mind was on. So next inning I'd shade the outfield and the ball would be hit to left, exactly where he said it would be hit. Or he'd say, 'We ought to bunt on this pitcher, he's out of position on his delivery,' and I'd call for the bunt and our man would damn near make it to second base after laying it down. In 1972, Dick Allen piloted the Chicago White Sox club as much as I did. We were co-managers."

Now, all this sounds pretty good, but with all the pre–White Sox episodes in the Ballplayer's career, I can't help but wonder aloud to Tanner if time has perhaps colored his memory about Allen's years under his regime. Wasn't it true, for instance, that Allen didn't have to abide by the same rules as the other players on that White Sox team?

"Guys would write that I had one set of rules for twenty-four players and a different set of rules for Dick Allen. Not true. I had twenty-five sets of rules. I took every player case by case and still do.

"On that '72 Sox team we had a number of veterans — Wilbur Wood, Bill Melton, and Carlos May, for example. I gave them all their freedom. My managing philosophy was a simple one — communication, not regimentation. But the media — as was always the case with Dick Allen — didn't see the bigger picture. Most guys need to abide by rules. Without them they'd fall apart, get out of shape, become lazy and undisciplined. Dick was a creative type of person. Not your typical ballplayer. I knew if I tried to box him in, I wouldn't get results. He'd be unhappy and so would I. Besides, you don't treat a man with the baseball skills and intelligence of a Dick Allen like an ordinary baseball player.

"To win, I needed Dick right beside me, helping me. I never worried about whether he took batting practice or not. I knew he'd always do what he thought was best for him and the team."

Solid. But how about blow-ups? No Tanner-Allen run-ins the whole season? No boozy confrontations? No disciplinary actions? No missed curfews? No clubhouse friction?

"Well, there was this one time," Tanner tells me, fixing his gaze to center field, where a number of his Atlanta pitchers are lazily shagging fly balls. "One morning I came out to the ballpark early and found Dick taking laps around the outfield. He was wearing a rubber suit and a weight belt and he was drenched in sweat. I asked one of the guys around the park how long he'd been out there. Turns out he had been out there two hours, taking batting practice, fielding grounders at first, doing wind sprints — and this was a morning after he had hit two home runs the night before. He wanted to win that badly. I said, 'Dick, you've got tonight off. In fact, take two nights off. Don't suit up.' He kicked and complained, but I insisted. That was the only time I disciplined Dick Allen. I gave him two days off and ordered him to rest."

It is nearing game time, so I close my notebook and begin

to thank Tanner for his help, but before I can finish he locks my arm under his elbow one last time and leans in close. "You know, it's important that baseball never forget Dick Allen," he says, speaking to me again in hushed, reverential tones. "Especially in Chicago. What Dick Allen accomplished in 1972 was very special. The owners of the White Sox should build a monument to Dick Allen in Comiskey Park, and they should do it today, right now, and they should put it in center field, where everybody can see it. Most people, when they think of the White Sox, they think of guys like Minnie Minoso and Nellie Fox, good ballplayers, but they never came close to having the kind of season Dick had in 1972. In my mind, Allen was the greatest White Sox player to ever wear the uniform."

Every time I try to get the Ballplayer to tell me about that glorious season of '72, clearly the single-season pinnacle of his fifteen-year baseball career, I find myself struggling with him to maintain a fluid dialogue. When I broach the subject of '72 in a linear fashion, Allen acts uninterested. Over the course of our eighteen months of collaboration, the Ballplayer has willingly talked to me about all aspects of both his baseball and personal life. And yet about 1972, he remains closed. Then it hits me: it's easier for Allen to talk to me about the dark days of his career; about those days, the Ballplayer can be analytical, introspective, even self-critical. But 1972 was an unabashed triumph for the Ballplayer. For Allen to talk about 1972, it would mean he'd have to talk about his personal triumphs — not a Dick Allen character trait. Insofar as 1972 is concerned, numbers speak. So I back off and wait. And eventually, over time, I learn about 1972, in classic Dick Allen riffs.

One day, while motoring in Los Angeles, the topic is spring training: "My favorite spring was '72. That was the year we were locked out of camp because Marvin Miller was doing battle over pension rights. But I had already arrived in Sarasota for spring training. My kind of timing. A lot of players on other teams around the leagues went home. But I stayed down, and so did a lot of the other players on the White Sox. We gigged every day. Worked on the fundamentals early in the morning, then chose up sides and played ball all afternoon. No media, no fans, just a bunch of ballplayers working hard, having fun. By the time the season started in June, we were in great shape and playing loose and happy baseball. Maybe we weren't the best team in baseball, but by the time the season got started we were ready. We were a happy, united baseball team."

Another day, over a couple of cold ones in St. Louis, the Ballplayer is remembering his first day as a White Sox: "There was a press conference, naturally. Whenever I was traded to a new team the front office would set up a press conference. I was always good box office, and management knew it. It was like a circus, and I was the main attraction. The first question I got in Chicago was 'What shall we call you, Rich, Richie, or Dick?' Know how many times I heard that? So I said what I always said: 'I prefer to be called Dick, but I just want to be a winner.'

"So next day, I open the Chicago papers and there I am — 'Dick Allen.' I go to the park, and everybody's calling me Dick — the ushers, the clubhouse guys, the fans. First time. First city to call me by the name my mother gave me at birth. I'd about given up. I made up my mind right then and there that Dick Allen was going to pay back Chicago for the respect they were giving me."

In Chicago, after a rare baseball card/memorabilia appearance, the subject turns to the '72 Oakland A's: "The A's were talented but unhappy. They hated their owner, Charlie Finley. That's why I felt we could beat their ass, even though we were just a bunch of scrappers. When we'd play the A's and one of their guys would reach first base, I'd get an earful about Finley. Especially from Reggie. He'd start talking about how cheap Charlie Finley was — the cattle car flights, no meal money, no food in the clubhouse. In my mind, Finley treated his players like second-class citizens because he was second-class himself. For a while that worked in our favor, but by September the A's were united in their loathing of Finley. Once they were all united, they began playing for each other, not for their owner. The A's became a team that season just in time to dash ahead of us to first place."

In a tavern outside of Wampum, the subject is Chuck Tanner: "I've always hated when people say Chuck was the only manager who knew how to handle me. Chuck didn't try to handle me. He didn't worry about whether I took batting practice or signed autographs or appeared on postgame shows. He understood the game was on the diamond. My question is, why didn't other managers feel the same way? Mauch was worried that I was undermining his authority, Schoendienst was always waiting for me to suddenly stop showing up, and Alston wanted me to bleed Dodger Blue. Then I get to Chuck, and all he cared about was winning ballgames. He knew how ball was played in Wampum. When I got to Chicago I told him everything I knew about baseball and he told me to go out and win."

But it was in Philadelphia, on a trip home to visit his three kids, that the Ballplayer may have spoken most directly about his achievements in 1972: "It was the pitching, man. Softer. In that National League, they would whiz one behind my ear at least one time every game. I got hit in the head once in the minors, and it's something you don't forget. The knock-down, the brushback, the in-your-ear hard one, call it what you want, I saw them all. That's how they deal with power in the National League. Try to scare you. It would, too. But you don't show it. You get mad instead. Gibson on the mound. *War.* Drysdale on the mound. *War.* Marichal on the mound. *War.* Then I get to the American League and what do I see? Curveball, curveball, fastball, back to curveball. Easy rhythm to read, and no threat of a concussion. Hey, baby! I just sat back and waited. I knew I'd get that fastball sooner or later right where I wanted it. I loved playing that year in Chicago. I still think of how it made me feel to drive into the South Side to do my thing. To feel that tingle. To feel all that love from the people of Chicago. But I got to say it: Compared to the National League, the American League is the pussy league of baseball."

Following that 1972 season, Allen was named the American League's Most Valuable Player. He won in a landslide vote, getting 21 first-place votes out of 24 cast by a special committee of the Baseball Writers' Association. In accepting the award, the Ballplayer was gracious. He thanked his teammates, the people of Chicago, and Chuck Tanner, the White Sox manager. Then he left, leaving the MVP award behind, where it sat in the White Sox training room gathering dust for years afterward.

Life had never looked more promising for the Ballplayer following that sensational '72 season. After being named

MVP, he signed a three-year $250,000 per annum contract with the White Sox, making him the highest-paid player in the game. What's more, the White Sox announced the Ballplayer's record-breaking contract with glee, noting that in 1972, Sox attendance had soared to 1,186,018, up from an abysmal 833,891 the season before. The Sox impressive 55–23 record at home was also noted. Sox general manager Roland Hemond minced no words in announcing the Ballplayer's pricey pact: "Dick Allen is responsible for saving the Sox franchise. Period."

The spring of '73, Allen reported to the Sox upbeat and anxious for another run at the flag.

Then, chasing a softly hit ball down the first-base line in a game against the Angels that June, Allen inadvertently leaped into the path of Mike Epstein, a 230-pound former college fullback. The collision was thunderous. When the dust settled, the Ballplayer found himself on the disabled list with a hairline fracture of the leg. He would return briefly five weeks later, his leg still broken, and actually go three for five, but the pain returned, and the Ballplayer was finished for the season.

"That injury set a lot of negative things in motion," Allen says of his post-'72 White Sox years.

Trouble started when the White Sox dismissed team doctor Hank Crawford at the start of the '74 season. Angry about his firing, Crawford lashed out at the White Sox in general and Allen in particular. He accused the Ballplayer of being a malingerer and claimed that Allen had been well enough to return to the active roster.

It was yet one more accusation in the Ballplayer's career that still disturbs Allen. "He didn't know anything about that injury because I didn't consult with him. I got that leg better the same way I got my hand better — with hard work, by myself, with no doctors around to make things worse. I lived to play ball. It was eating me alive not to be able to play. Then I got to hear that jive. He was angry because the Sox fired him, and maybe if I had allowed him to work with me he might have seemed more useful. But that's not the way I heal. I heal alone."

There was also the issue of Hank Allen, the Ballplayer's older brother. Hank joined the Sox at the end of the '72 season at the age of thirty-two. A lifetime .241 hitter who had played most of his seven seasons with the hapless Washington Senators, Hank Allen was at the close of an undistinguished career. When the Ballplayer was in the midst of his MVP season, his brother's presence on the roster was not an issue. But now, with Dick on the disabled list, people began to wonder aloud about Hank Allen's qualifications. At the start of the '73 season, brother Hank needed just eighty-two days on a big league roster to qualify for a major league pension. Some said that Tanner had signed Hank Allen under pressure to placate brother Dick.

"Damn right I wanted Hank to get that pension. He's my brother. I mentioned to the Sox how close he was to getting those days under his belt. Chuck said, 'Let's bring Hank home with that pension, Dick.' That was it. Hank didn't have the same skills I had on the baseball field. But he had the same desire. He was a good guy to have on a team. His desire to win would infect the rest of the guys on the pine."

Dick Allen on the 1974 season:

Things never felt right with the White Sox in '74 from the start. I felt confused, disoriented, but mostly depressed. My baseball career was slipping through my fingers, and it was getting harder to see where I was going to get a ring for my efforts.

That March, I was in a batting cage, working by myself against a mechanical pitching device. I was trying to get my stroke back after the '73 layoff. Next thing I know Will Grimsley, an AP writer, comes up to me out of nowhere, and he starts asking me for an interview. I begged him, I said, "Man, I'm just trying to do my job. Leave me be." But he wouldn't stop asking me questions. Finally, I said, "Here, here's fifty bucks, just leave me the hell be." So he gets all outraged and writes a column saying I was a public figure and that meant I should be nice to him. Bullshit, man. And the same old bullshit. I was beginning to get those old-time bad vibes.

I had become the White Sox team leader, not by choice, believe me, it just came my way by playing hard, leading by example. I had a lot of fun that year. But in '74, the Sox went and got Ron Santo from the Cubs. Things got real screwed up both on the field and in the clubhouse after that. Santo thought himself a Chicago institution because he had played all those years across town with the Cubs. He thought he should be the team leader automatically. But you don't get to be a leader through longevity. Santo had all our guys screwed up.

In '72, I had been working a lot with a second baseman named Jorge Orta. When Jorge came to us that year he was just a scared twenty-two-year-old kid from Mexico. He was a sensitive kid, reminded me of myself. I worked on that boy's confidence, quietly, picking the right spots to build him up and the right time to let him know when he screwed up. Now here comes Santo, acting the grizzled veteran, barking at everyone and rattling everybody's cage.

One day Orta boots a grounder at second, and I overhear Santo yelling at him from third. I get hot.

Between innings, I call Santo over. "Hey, my man," I say to him. "How long you been in the big leagues?"

"Fourteen years," he tells me.

"You ever screw up over those fourteen years?"

"Yeah," he says.

I point to Orta. "Well, that boy right there — this is his third season in the big leagues. He's still learning. But he's going to be a good one. You got a lot to teach. Instead of yelling at Georgie, why don't you teach him a few things?"

Santo doesn't say anything. He just sneers at me.

After that, I had no time for Santo. Baseball is a game to be passed on from veterans to kids — at least that's the way I saw it. Santo was in his last big league season. He was feeling washed up and it showed.

The tension between Santo and me began to spread to the other guys in the clubhouse. We stopped being a team. I was still hitting the ball, and hitting it good. But we weren't winning — and we weren't having fun. Then one day Chuck came up to me and told me the dissension was ruining the team. He said, "There's only room for one guy to run this team — and that's me." That's when I knew things would never be the same. I decided it was time to go home.

On September 14, 1974, near the end of his third season with the White Sox, the Ballplayer gathered his White Sox teammates together in the clubhouse. At the time he was hitting .302 and leading the American League in home runs with 32. In one week in June of '74, the Ballplayer had averaged better than a double in each of his twelve hits, for an aggregate of 22 total bases. His RBIs in those eight games were 4, 4, 2, 0, 3, 2, 2, 0, a total of 17 runs batted in. In his two and a half seasons in the American League, he had smoked 85 home runs.

But despite the numbers, he had decided to announce his retirement.

There wasn't a sound in the room as Allen began to speak:

This is hard for me to say. I've never been happier anywhere but here. You're still going to be a good ballclub without me. You've got a good manager in this guy . . .

The Ballplayer pointed to Chuck Tanner, his manager, then broke down in tears. He tried to speak again, twice, then a third time, but each time he was unable to regain his composure.

Without saying anything else, the Ballplayer walked out of the Sox clubhouse and returned to his farm in Philadelphia.

•9•

Crash Redux

Dick Allen on the Philadelphia years, 1975–1976:

I was chilling out on my farm in Pennsylvania in the spring of '75 when I got a visit from Mike Schmidt, Dave Cash, and Richie Ashburn. At the time Schmidt and Cash were both playing for the Phillies, and Ashburn was a member of the Phillies broadcasting team. I always was one to be hospitable, especially to baseball guys, so I had Barbara barbecue up some ribs, I tapped us a keg, and we all sat around and talked some baseball.

It was a conversation I wouldn't forget. Schmidt was talking about how the Phils needed some additional clout, a big stick in the lineup to go with his and Greg Luzinski's. He said something about Schmidt/Luzinski/Allen firepower. Cash was rapping about the brothers on the Phils team and how they could use a veteran to inspire them. And ol' Richie Ashburn was telling tales about how much the city of Philadelphia had changed for the better. That was about as specific as it got, but I got the message:

Come home, Dick. We love you, Rich. They're gonna love you, Richie.

At first I figured it had to be a joke. It's not my style to return to the scene of the crime. But I had to admit the idea of coming home did fire me up a bit. I always did like surprises — even when the surprises were on me. When they left the farm that day, I hugged them all. I was touched to feel wanted by guys who played for the Phillies. But, like I say, no specific requests were made, and no promises were given.

Two days later, I got another visit, this time from Ashburn and Robin Roberts, the old Phillies Hall of Famer. Things were getting a bit serious now.

Then, a couple of days after that visit, I opened the *Philadelphia Inquirer* and there it was: KUHN INVESTIGATING PHILS FOR TAMPERING WITH ALLEN.

Just like the old days. I was home already.

When I left the Sox near the end of the '74 season I fully intended to follow through with retirement. I'd been injured six times, and each one had taken its toll. I was hurting physically and mentally. I'd been through Little Rock, Frank Thomas, Gene Mauch, Bob Skinner, Ron Santo, and too many close pennant races with no ring to show for it. When I walked out of that Chicago White Sox clubhouse, it cost me $25,000. But I never was one to be a slave to money.

When I came home to my Pennsylvania farm, I had one thing in mind: raising horses. I had thirteen acres of beautiful countryside in the prettiest state in the nation. On the farm we had a rambling house, a red barn big enough to take care of thirteen fine horses, and enough privacy to make even me a happy man.

With baseball behind me, I was hopeful I could get my

relationship with Barbara back on track. We had been through a lot together since making things legal in '64. She had stood by me through a lot of dark days. We had three children together — Teri, my oldest daughter, Dickie Jr., and my youngest boy, who we called Button. I had been away from my family during my baseball days. Barbara had been there when I couldn't be. I was hoping to make amends.

But things between Barbara and me seemed to get worse with my being home all the time. Baseball does bad things to marriages. The truth is that most ballplayers use their wives as checkpoints during their careers — somebody to come home to, somebody to take care of the bills. Then when it's all over, they come home and nobody can adjust. The wife, the ballplayer, they look at each other and say, "Now what?"

Barbara and I couldn't see eye to eye on horses. Horses take work, a lot of work. You have to get up with them at dawn, feed them, clean them, exercise them. Barbara began to feel like she was being held hostage on the farm. There was a lot of resentment. She used to say it wasn't a normal life. She wanted to go out more. I told her what I told her the day we got married: that the three most important things in my life are God, my mother, and baseball — and everything else comes after that.

As things grew worse between us, I got closer to my horses. I've always gotten along better with horses than with people. My horses communicated with me about everything. On the farm they would tell me when somebody was coming. Their ears would stand straight up in the air even when the person coming to visit was in a car three miles away. If it was a sportswriter, the horses would start

kicking up a storm. They knew to warn me when somebody
was coming that I didn't want to see. That would give me
time to get out of sight.

That March, my dad died. It's not easy for me to talk
about him and what he meant to me. He wasn't around
much when I was growing up, but he had a profound effect
on me. When I went to his funeral, I felt on the verge of
collapse. I had kept so many of my feelings about my father
buried inside me. That was Mother's way, and I guess I
tried to do it her way. I was a lot like my father, that I
know. I was strong like my father physically, and head-
strong like him too. It was very hard for me to cope with his
death, and it still is today.

With my father gone and things so bad in my marriage,
I began to think seriously about playing baseball again.
Also I needed the bread. Horses are expensive. They cost
a lot to feed, a lot to maintain. I used to buy horses to race
them at the track. But I was never hardhearted about my
horses, and you have to be hard if you're going to make
money with horses at the track. If one of my horses was
hurting, I'd nurse him back to health. A lot of horse
trainers just believe in running the race, no matter. There's
a lot of cruelty in the horse business, and it used to break
my heart to see a hurting horse get pushed. To keep my
horses going, I would need money. And since I always was
able to make money hitting a baseball, I began to rethink
things again.

Then came those visits from the Phillies.

The idea of playing again in Philadelphia, as unlikely as it
seemed, was growing on me. Richie Ashburn had talked a
lot of sense to me on that visit. He was one man I could

trust. He had played a lot of baseball in Philadelphia, going all the way back to the 1950 Phillies Whiz Kids. A damn fine ballplayer, good glove, steady hit, good speed, a Hall of Famer in my book. He was also a very honest man. Ashburn told me that when Jackie Robinson came up to the major leagues, he was one of the players in the league who was most against him. Being from Nebraska, he had never been around black people before Jackie. But Ashburn turned completely around on the question of race. He told me how he had come to admire the way black folks played the game. When things were really raining down on me in Philadelphia, Ashburn was one of the few outspoken voices in that city on my behalf. I saw him as a living example of how people can change. I began to convince myself that maybe a whole city could change too.

But before I could think about playing for the Phillies, there was the little matter of who owned me — or who thought they owned me. When I left the Sox, I never did turn in an official retirement letter to the American League. I never did believe in messing with unnecessary paperwork. So what did the Sox do? Sold me to the Atlanta Braves — and for chump change, about five grand. When I heard that, I called up Roland Hemond, the general manager of the White Sox, and told him I was giving some thought to playing again. Would the Sox be interested? He said, "Good to hear you want to play, Dick. You'll like Atlanta."

Like I always say — and this is a Dick Allen message to all young ballplayers: Grab the paper when you can, brothers, 'cause baseball has no memory, no heart, no soul. And it goes away quick.

I made up my mind about Atlanta real quick — I wasn't going. No southern hospitality for me. Not after what I had been through in Florida during my early spring training years — all those springs having to stay in run-down boarding houses and eating in separate restaurants. And all I had been through in Little Rock. I had also heard that Clyde King, the manager of the Braves and a native Southerner, was not what you'd call an equal opportunity employer. Atlanta just wasn't for me. Look what Atlanta had done to Henry Aaron, the greatest home run hitter of all time. People forget it now, but when Aaron was going for those 715 master-blasters there were people rooting *against* him in his own home ballpark! Henry Aaron. Baseball's most distinguished gentleman. I could just imagine what they'd have in store for me.

The Braves got the message, because the next thing I knew they had made a deal with the Phillies right after Bowie Kuhn made his decision to dismiss the tampering charges. The Phillies gave the Braves a player and some cash for the right to sign me. With that out of the way, I met with Ruly Carpenter, who was Bob Carpenter's son and by now the man in charge of the club. Ruly was a lot like his dad. He had a lot of money, old money, but he also had integrity. Ruly talked to me about winning a flag. Then I talked to Danny Ozark, the Phillies manager. I knew Danny was skeptical. He had been a coach under Alston with the Dodgers when I had played there. He admired my talent and skills on the field, but Danny was a company man. He knew I didn't always toe the company line. But he did want to win a pennant.

Earlier that winter, while I was deciding what to do, the *Philadelphia Daily News* conducted a poll of readers about me. They called it "Love Him or Leave Him." The result was that 1,531 fans voted to love me; 887 voted to leave me.

Almost two to one in my favor. Damn near blew me away.

I reported to the team in June. I had missed a month of baseball in '74 and now the first two months of '75. I needed to work my way back. But Ozark told me the press was on him to use me. The first day I walked into the Phillies clubhouse, Bob Carpenter was waiting there to greet me. He stuck out his hand and said, "Welcome home, son." I could feel tears filling my eyes.

My first time up as the Phillies' Prodigal Son, I got a standing ovation. I singled to left and got another standing ovation. Ashburn had been right: Things had changed.

For one thing, the Phillies were now playing in Veterans Stadium. It was a totally different atmosphere than what I had experienced at old Connie Mack Stadium. The Vet was big and modern, and the fans were farther away from the action. There was turf instead of grass. The fans were different, too. In the old stadium the crowd was racially mixed, and that created a lot of tension. But here the crowd was suburban — and white. When the Phillies moved out of North Philadelphia to white South Philadelphia, they lost their black fans. I remember looking up and wondering where all the brothers had gone.

There was another difference, too: Times had changed. In the sixties, racial tensions in Philadelphia were always at the boiling point. Frank Rizzo, who had been the city's police commissioner and later the mayor, would say and do things that divided the city racially. He once raided the headquarters of the Black Panthers in North Philadelphia and strip-searched the brothers he found inside. The newspapers ran pictures of them lined up against the wall bare-assed. Now blacks were beginning to run the city. In the old days, I represented a threat to white people in Philadelphia. I wore my hair in an Afro. I said what was on my mind. I didn't take shit. But now, like the rest of the country, Philadelphia had come around to accepting that things had changed and were going to keep changing, like it or not.

The Phillies organization had also entered the twentieth century, though it was still behind most of the teams in baseball in terms of racial equality. The brothers on the team — Dave Cash, Ollie Brown, and Garry Maddox — represented a new generation of black ballplayer. They were talented and proud of it, and they didn't take a back seat to anybody.

In terms of pure baseball, I looked around that clubhouse and liked what I saw. We had Schmitty at third base, and there was no telling what he could do, Cash at second, Bowa at short, Bob Boone behind the plate, me at first. Pretty tough infield. We had Luzinski and Maddox in the outfield, and platooners Ollie Brown and Mike Anderson to round it out. We had pitchers like Steve Carlton and Jim Lonborg, and Tug McGraw and Gene Garber in the bullpen. I remember thinking that maybe with this bunch I could get myself a World Series ring after all.

It didn't take me long to realize that 1975 wasn't going to be my kind of year at the plate. The layoff had hurt me, and I couldn't find my groove all year. I felt that Ozark had put me in the lineup before I was ready. I had tried to tell him that, but he didn't want to hear it. He told me the press was on him to get me in there.

Once I realized I wasn't going to be able to contribute my usual numbers, I took a different tack. I began to teach.

Not just technique, but style. I had picked up a lot about the game in twelve years in the bigs, and I figured it was time to pass it on. I never offered, unless asked, but lots of guys asked. With Luzinski, it was a question of teaching him how to become a zone hitter. The Bull was all clout, but he swung at a lot of bad pitches. He was a low-ball hitter. He could drive a low pitch a mile, but on high pitches he looked like the fat kid in school who never learned to play the game. I would talk to him about patience. You've got to wait for your pitch, Bull, I would tell him. You have to know your strengths. I also told him a secret that I had kept to myself for years.

Never think home run. Always think two-base hit.

Luzinski had a hell of a year in '75. He hit .300 and smacked 34 home runs.

Schmidt was a different kind of challenge. He had as much talent as anybody I've ever seen play the game. Quick wrists. Strong. Perfect baseball body. But he was trying to hit every pitch out of the park, and when he didn't he'd sulk about it. When I got to Philly in '75, he didn't seem to like playing the game.

I talked to him about swinging down on the ball. One of the biggest myths in baseball is that the way to play clout ball is to uppercut. Just the opposite. The downswing gives the ball more velocity when you make contact. Balls hit with the downswing will start as line drives, but will gather momentum and end up leaving the park. I learned that from my brother Coy, who learned it himself from playing in the Negro Leagues. The downswing is the ticket, baby. Schmidt picked up on it pretty quick.

The other thing about Schmidt was his attitude. He was moody, and if he had a bad game he'd take it home with him. I used to take him out after a game for a couple of beers and we'd talk about things, have a few laughs, put the ballyard behind us. I used to tell Schmitty to pretend he was back in the sandlots of Ohio where he grew up. Get out there and bang that ball like you did in high school. He began to get the message. He hit 38 home runs in '75 but struggled with his average. He still had some work to do.

We finished in second place in the National League East in '75, behind the Pirates. I finished with a .233 average and only 12 home runs. But there were other factors that hurt me that season. One, I was hitting behind the Bull, which didn't give me many options. Bull was a disaster on the base paths. I couldn't play hit-and-run, couldn't sacrifice, couldn't bunt him over. All I could do was go up whacking. I did manage to knock home 62 runs — no easy task when you figure that the Bull batted in 120 runs himself hitting ahead of me. On paper, I wasn't an All-Star, but on balance I was pretty pleased with my accomplishments in '75.

In the spring of 1976, almost a year to the month after I lost my father, I drove Clem Capozzoli, my friend and unofficial agent, to the Tampa airport so he could catch a plane for Philadelphia. Clem never made the plane. He died of a heart attack in the airport. He was fifty-nine.

Though people used to say that Clem was a father figure in my life, I never believed it until he died. Then I knew it was true. Any money I gave him I had to force on him. He got me to do all kinds of things that no other man could have ever made me do. He had kept me in the game many times when I wanted to quit. I took his loss hard and decided I would dedicate the '76 season to his memory.

Through the first two-thirds of the '76 season, we were

red hot. In early August we were coasting along in the NL East with a 15½ game lead. But then things started to unravel. On Labor Day we lost both ends of a doubleheader to the Pirates, and that reduced our lead to 5½ games with 26 to go. All of a sudden the Bucs were on our ass. While we were losing 10 of our last 11 games, the Pirates were winning 12 of 13.

The newspapers began making comparisons to '64. I was the guy who had been there, and I *knew* this wasn't '64. We were just tired. I knew our talent would surface in time. We were scrappers in '64, but this '76 team had oomph. With Schmidt, the Bull, and me the lineup, things weren't going to stay quiet for long.

I had been going real bad, 3 for 40 in the late August stretch. Finally, Ozark sat me down. I'll never forget it. He sat me for an entire three-game series against the Cubs. It was the first time I'd been benched in my life. After the Cubs series, he put me back in the lineup in a game against the Cardinals. John Denny was the pitcher. I hit two doubles and a home run. It got us back on track.

Afterward, Ozark got a lot of credit for snapping me out of that slump. He may have deserved it. I can take all kinds of things, but sitting on the bench while a baseball game is being played in front of me is not one of them.

We were on our way to clinching our division, but internally I could sense trouble coming. I was starting to get an uneasy feeling about things. Ollie Brown — we called him "Downtown" — was being platooned with Jerry Martin in left field, and a lot of us felt he should have been given the job. Bobby Tolan was another guy who wasn't getting the shot he deserved. There was a sense that the Phillies were working a quota on us, and the clubhouse started getting divided because of it. We were starting to feel like two teams, black and white, though Schmitty was an honorary black. He seemed to understand what was going on. He was also sporting an Afro at the time, even if it was a bright red one.

There were other forces at work too. Larry Bowa was always making noise. Hollering at umpires and generally being an outspoken pain in the ass. He always had something to say, and it was never helpful. He told a writer that he missed having Willie Montanez playing first base because Willie could dig the balls out of the dirt. Since I was the guy who replaced Montanez, the implication was clear: I couldn't. When I asked Bowa about it, he denied ever having said it. I said my piece anyway. I told him that Montanez had been a great-fielding first baseman — *so good* that Bowa had turned into a lazy shortstop. I told him to stand up and fire that ball to first like he meant it. Hit the damn target. I think he knew where I was coming from.

We also had Tug McGraw as one of our major character actors. I liked Tug all right, but I didn't like him in my face. He had played in New York with the Mets, so to him baseball was a Broadway play. He was always mugging for the cameras and getting himself as much attention as he could. Between Bowa and McGraw, we never had a moment of quiet.

Then, just before we clinched the division, the Phillies announced that they had to cut the squad back to twenty-five players and that Tony Taylor might be the one declared ineligible for both the playoffs and the World Series. We had played with twenty-six guys all year. Taylor and I had both played hurt. I had separated my shoulder in July running into John Candelaria down the first-base line.

When I went on the disabled list, Taylor would be the guy activated. When I came back, Taylor would be put on the DL. It was a strange arrangement, but we'd been doing it all season. Now they were saying he had to go.

To my way of thinking, nothing could be more unfair than for the Phillies to take Tony Taylor's uniform. Taylor had played nineteen seasons in the big leagues, but never in a World Series. He had been a model ballplayer in the Phillies organization, mostly through the club's worst times. He was the one guy that would walk to the box seats and sign autographs before every game. He was the one who would volunteer to do a postgame interview when the rest of us were turning our backs on the press. In all his years, he never complained. Tony Taylor was Philadelphia Phillies baseball.

Would they have done this to Richie Ashburn in a similar situation? Robin Roberts? The way I saw it, they were taking advantage of Taylor's disposition and race. I felt a personal stake in this. I had a great love for Tony Taylor. He had been my best man at my wedding. His son was born in the same delivery room of the same hospital where my son was born. We had spent a lot of hours talking baseball: Taylor had taught me baseball, Cuban style; I taught him brotherball.

When I heard that the Phillies were thinking about taking Taylor's uniform, I told the press exactly what I was going to do about it. "With God as my witness," I said, "if the Phillies take Tony Taylor's uniform off his back, they'll have to take Dick Allen's too."

In late September, we clinched the National League East. We won it in the first game of a doubleheader in Montreal. The celebration started immediately. In the clubhouse, guys were acting like we had won the World Series. Ozark was running around giving interviews to every television crew in sight. Tug McGraw was walking around bare-assed serving sandwiches. Larry Bowa was pouring champagne on heads and telling everybody what a happy little guy he was. I walked into the clubhouse, saw what was going on, and walked back out to the dugout and sat down. I said a prayer of thanks. I had been waiting a long time to be on a winner. But we had only won the division. We still had to play a series against the Reds in the National League West before we could even get to the Series.

When the second game started that day, I went into the clubhouse. A few of us — Cash, Schmitty, and Tolan — said a little prayer together and then we toasted with champagne.

After that doubleheader, the team headed for St. Louis. I headed for home. I was happy to be on a winner, but I was torn up about how I felt about the Phillies organization. My shoulder was hurting. I needed to mentally recharge for the playoffs. I was wearing down. I was thinking a lot about my father and about Clem and for the first time coming to grips with how both of these men had fit into my life. I was not getting along with Barbara at home. I was worried about my horses. I was short-circuiting.

The Phillies decided to let Tony Taylor stay in uniform for the championship series against the Reds, but as a coach, not as an active player. I felt that wasn't good enough. But Taylor came to me and insisted that I play — if he hadn't done that, I would have watched that series from an easy chair on my farm.

As it turned out, I may have been better off. The

Philadelphia fans were back on me for not making the trip to St. Louis after clinching the division. To them, it was the reemergence of Richie Allen. I began to get booed, and the threats started coming to me in the mail again. My mother heard what was going on in Philadelphia and decided that she wasn't coming to town to watch the playoffs. "I don't want to hear it, I don't want to see it," she told me over the phone just before the playoffs began. "I don't want to feel people hating my son."

We lost that five-game series to the Reds in three straight. We had beaten the Reds handily all season, but all the turmoil in the clubhouse over the final few weeks of the regular season had us feeling and playing like a broken team. I was blamed personally for losing the second game of that series. In that game, we were ahead, 2–1, the Reds had the bases loaded, and Tony Perez hit a line drive at me at first base. I threw up my glove but missed. It was ruled an error. The ball bounded into right field and the Reds scored two — and won the game.

I know to the average fan it appeared that I simply blew the play. But there were things happening on that play that the average fan didn't know about. What they didn't know was that the pickoff play was on. Bob Boone, our catcher, was going to gun it down to me at first. When the ball was hit at me, I was moving in the opposite direction. I threw up my glove anyway, out of desperation, but I was totally out of position. The strange thing about all this is that guys on the Reds saw what happened. After the game, Sparky Anderson and Joe Morgan both explained to the media why the ball should have been ruled a hit. Meanwhile, Danny Ozark was telling people that the ball should have been caught. He told the writers, "It's only one man's opinion,

but I say it should have been an out." I had to get out of
there. I knew if I stayed, Danny was going to catch one
man's opinion of *him* right on the chin.

Just prior to that dismal championship series, both
Danny Ozark and Ruly Carpenter made it clear to me that
there wouldn't be a place for me with the Phillies in '77.

They did wish me luck.

•10•

Life After Baseball

The following dialogue is based on conversations with Dick Allen, the Ballplayer, over an eighteen-month period.

The Writer: Tough way to end a career — playing for Charlie Finley's Oakland A's?

The Ballplayer: One last kick in the ass. After I left the Phillies in '76, I still felt like I had some ball in me. I was a baseball-a-holic. Finley was a renegade, and so was I. I thought it would be a good match. I played 54 games under Finley in '77, but then I began to see what the man was really like. He was a liar, as in l-i-a-r. Got that?

The Writer: How did he lie?

The Ballplayer: All ways, all day. The man was always working a scam. He said he was going to make us a winner. He was going to trade for this guy and that guy. Got me fired up. But all he did was make everybody feel like a loser. Before I joined the A's, I told Finley I wouldn't agree to being the team's designated hitter. As far as I was concerned, the DH was the worst thing that had happened to baseball in my lifetime. The game is meant to be played both offensively and defensively. Finley gave me his word.

We shook hands on it. Then, as soon as the season started, I began to get pressure to DH. I reached the end of the line with Finley early that summer. He came into the clubhouse in the sixth inning of a game in July. I was taking a shower. He said, "What are you doing?" I said, "Cooling down." What I didn't say was that I was sick of playing for a last-place team owned by a con man. Finley said, "Listen, Dick, I can't have you doing this. What's it going to look like?" Right then, I knew Finley didn't know me. I was never one to care what something looked like. So then Finley says, "I'm going to suspend you and tell the press it's without pay. But I'll pay you under the table. What do you say?" I told him, "Charlie, tell the truth — and keep the money." Then I left the clubhouse and went home. I was scheduled to join the team in Anaheim ten days later. But the suspension ended the Fourth of July weekend and I had a big softball game on the farm scheduled with my family and friends. I knew the softball game would be more fun — and probably more competitive than the ball we were playing in Oakland. So I stayed home. Cost me about two hundred grand to walk away, but it was worth every penny. That's how it ended.

The Writer: You stayed on the farm?

The Ballplayer: The farm and my horses. I worked with the horses from morning to night. I was hoping to build up my own stable of fine racehorses. But I still couldn't get ball out of my system. I thought about going to Japan. I got lots of offers. Good paper, too. But the game ain't the same there. You play in the Show for fifteen seasons, it gets hard to come down to a lower level. So instead I worked the stables from morning to night.

The Writer: Things got a little tough in the years immediately following baseball.

The Ballplayer: I knew we were going to get to that. October 11, 1979. I won't forget that date. I was downstairs watching TV in the main house on the farm. I'd been watching the World Series. I guess I fell asleep. Baseball on television always did make me nod out. Next thing I know I hear this loud explosion and flames started shooting out of the television. I ran upstairs to wake up Barbara and the kids. By the time I got them all up, there was smoke everywhere. We all got up on the roof, and luckily there was a ladder against the house. We had been having our roof repaired. We all got down safely. The firemen got there and hosed down what was left of the house. I had no insurance. The horses had eaten up all my money. The IRS was dogging me. I had hoped I could get away without insurance for a few months until we sold the place. I watched my whole life go up in smoke and felt numb. Afterward, they said the fire was a fluke, some kind of short in the electrical system.

The Writer: After the fire you disappeared for a while.

The Ballplayer: True. Got in Big Blue and just split. After the house burned down, me and Barbara and the kids, we all moved into a small house we had on the property for the men who worked the stables. I was depressed. I wasn't doing Barbara any good, I wasn't doing the kids any good, I wasn't doing myself any good. And there was no room to breathe. I was waiting for the next thing to happen — and when it did, I knew it wasn't going to be any good. I had to rebuild from scratch, and I went about doing it the way I've done everything my whole life — alone.

The Writer: What were you doing?

The Ballplayer: Trying to find myself, and moving around a lot. I got myself a crib in California. I also got myself back in touch with God. I did a lot of communicating. I read my Bible, got myself a new girlfriend. After a while, I started to see daylight.

The Writer: Was the divorce from Barbara difficult?

The Ballplayer: Difficult — and very expensive. There were a lot of bad feelings between us. She wanted me to be a husband and a father. I wanted her to understand what my baseball life had done to me. I also wanted Teri, Dickie, and Buttons to know, too. But Barbara had gathered them under her wing. She started a whole new life — and there was no room for Dick Allen in it. She went to court and got it all, including my pension. And she never once had to stand in against a Bob Gibson fastball. That's what's unfair.

The Writer: Do you see the kids today?

The Ballplayer: When I can. All three are good-looking and college-educated. My oldest, Teri, she's just out of college and looking for a career in broadcasting. My youngest, Buttons, he's a junior in college and talks about getting into international finance — I wish he had been into that during my playing days. My middle boy, Dickie Jr., wants to play ball like his old man. He loves the game. He works in Philadelphia's Veterans Stadium with the grounds crew. He'll do anything to be around ball. It scares me to see how much he loves baseball.

The Writer: I know Dick Jr. has had tryouts with big league clubs.

The Ballplayer: Yes, and it hasn't been easy for him. He's got my name, and that has made life difficult. Guy comes to look at him, and right away he's thinking, "Can he clout like the old man?" Dickie Jr. doesn't play clout ball — he plays the whole game. Runs well, fields well, sprays the ball around the outfield. A damn fine prospect. But he can't get anybody to take a chance with him, and I can't understand it. He's got all this ingrained baseball knowledge. I called one scout about him, and he said, "Dick, I'd love to sign the boy, but I just can't." I said, "What the hell do you mean, you *can't?*" But he wouldn't answer. It's one thing for *me* to be blackballed from baseball — but my son?

The Writer: There were rumors, and even some things written in the newspapers, that after the fire and your divorce from Barbara, drink got the best of you.

The Ballplayer: Yeah, I heard that, and it came from the same guys who used to say the other things about me — the writers. The stories about me change, but the people who say them don't. I like to have fun, enjoy a couple of cold green ones as much as the next guy. But it's become a big overblown story, this Dick Allen and drinking story.

The Writer: Rehab clinics are filled with current and former professional athletes.

The Ballplayer: I think there should be more pressure put on parents to make sure things don't go haywire early. That's where the addiction starts. A family shouldn't have to put up with the shame of seeing one of their own check into a rehab clinic while the whole world watches. If I ever thought I needed that kind of help, I would go home to my mother. I'd go right back to Wampum. There I could get all the love I'd need to beat back whatever it was that was hurting me.

The Writer: Do you stay in touch with guys from your playing days?

The Ballplayer: The friends you make in baseball are for life. I still see Orlando Cepeda, a fellow outlaw. Fought all the way back. I see Fergie Jenkins. I drop in on Johnny Callison when I'm around Philly. I still see Gibson — he's the same, still looking to stick it in somebody's ear. I stay in touch with Aaron. Lots of guys. I may not see any of them every week, but when we get together we get down to cases. There's hardly a man that pulled on the uniform that I wouldn't call a friend — Gene Mauch included.

The Writer: I know you were once close to Bob Uecker.

The Ballplayer: Ueck? Still busts me up. Saw him in an airport recently and when he saw me he said, "Je-sus Christ! If it ain't Richie Allen, the baddest bleepty-bleep to ever play the game!" Ran right for me and gave me a bear hug. A lot of guys I played with in baseball thought they were funny, but Ueck really was funny. Tickled me like nobody else in the game. We were sitting together in an airplane once, back when we were teammates in Philly, and just to liven things up a bit Ueck asked the stewardess for a barf bag. Tells her he feels sick. She gives him the bag and when she turns her back, he makes this big noise like he's vomiting. The whole time he's making the noise he's pouring a big can of Campbell's clam chowder into the bag. Except I'm the only one who can see him do it. When the stewardess comes back, he asks her for a spoon and starts eating the stuff out of the bag. Guys started running for the bathroom.

The Writer: I know your closest friend outside the game is Angel Cordero, Jr., the jockey.

The Ballplayer: Yeah, baby. Outside or inside. And let me say my piece about him. Angel is the baddest jock to ever climb a horse. And yet with all his records and all his winnings, he doesn't get the play of a Willie Shoemaker. He doesn't get the big commercial spots or the big magazine stories. Why? Skin color, one. Two, he doesn't play by the same rules as the establishment jocks. The people who run the horse industry are the same type of folks who own baseball clubs. Sometimes the very same people. Angel does it his way. And he's broken nearly every bone in his body doing it. Yet there he is — riding, riding, riding. Angel's a good friend. Over the years, we've picked each other up in tough times. Angel's a genuine soulmate.

The Writer: Do you like California living?

The Ballplayer: I do — when I'm here. I stay in California when Santa Anita's in season. I get there early and watch the horses go through their workouts. It clears my head. When the season ends, I usually jump in Big Blue and head for the open road. I still move around a lot. Still got the gypsy in my soul.

The Writer: Do you miss the game?

The Ballplayer: I love the game. If I see a baseball game when I'm motoring cross country in Big Blue, I'll pull over and watch a few innings. The game is a beautiful thing to watch. I especially like watching kids on a diamond. Nothing is sweeter than watching young athletic bodies execute a fluid double play.

The Writer: Do you miss being in the game?

The Ballplayer: If you mean being in the Show, no. If you mean being part of the game itself, yes. Major league baseball sold out a long time ago. I don't sell out, mostly because I don't know how.

The Writer: How did baseball sell out?

The Ballplayer: When I was a kid they always played the World Series during the day. In Wampum, everybody worked shift work. Guys could work their schedules so they could at least see some of the Series. Now, with the Series played at night, the guys working nights are shut out. I loved major league baseball when it was the workingman's game. Baseball was unifying to these men. Now, it's all played at nighttime because television wants the prime-time market. But what major league baseball doesn't realize is that the guys that work during the day get tired at night, and if the game is boring — click — they're off to bed.

The Writer: What do you miss most about your playing days?

The Ballplayer: Being part of the baseball family. For fifteen years, I ate with twenty-five guys, worked with twenty-five guys, partied with twenty-five guys. Then, all of a sudden — whoosh — I'm on my own. I miss going out and trying to win one. I miss the competition.

The Writer: You spent some time in the horse business with your brothers Hank and Ronnie for a few years immediately following your baseball days.

The Ballplayer: Hank and Ronnie were both able to make the switch from the baseball business to the horse business easily. I helped them get started — and I'm proud of them. Today, they've got themselves one of the most successful stables in the country just outside Laurel, Maryland. Maybe because they didn't have as much success in baseball — Ronnie only played seven games in the bigs — it made it easier for them to make the transition. Tough for me. I've never been able to think about the horse business in the same way as my brothers. When I go to visit them in Maryland, first place I go is to the stables to say hello to the horses. Soon as I walk in, the horses get all excited. I say, "Hey fellas, what's shakin'?" and they all start wagging their tails and getting themselves all worked up. I love the horses for who they are, but the buying and selling of them is something I've never been very good at. And contrary to a lot of rumors, I've never been much of a gambler.

The Writer: Do you feel bitter about baseball?

The Ballplayer: At one time I did. Immediately after I left the game I would sit around and feel sorry for myself. Wonder why it couldn't have gone differently. All those years I played I never once met anybody who loved the game as much as I did. I couldn't figure out why baseball didn't love me back. But I don't feel that way anymore. When I go around to some of these old-timers' games now and see all the guys, I see how much they care for me. And I realize how much I care about them. I guess I'd forgotten that. I wish I could say that baseball's been very, very good to me. But there were times when it wasn't. But that's okay. What's done is done.

The Writer: How do you feel about Philadelphia?

The Ballplayer: It's home. I love Philly. I want Philly to love me. I hope that someday the fans there realize how much I wanted to win a flag for them. I would have done anything to bring it home for them. I think somewhere they know that.

The Writer: You have flirted with baseball a bit since your retirement — first with the Texas Rangers, then with the White Sox.

The Ballplayer: Ol' Don Zimmer asked me to come down and give him a hand in spring training with the Rangers in '81. I enjoyed it, but I felt like a fool wearing that uniform without being able to gig myself. After spring training, he asked me to join the team as a coach for the season. I thought about it, but I didn't want to wear the uniform unless I could get my licks. Hurts too much to be in uniform and not be able to play. Then, in '86, Hawk Harrelson — he was then the general manager of the White Sox — asked me to work with Kenny Williams, one of their prospects on the farm. That I enjoyed. I followed him around on the minor league circuit, gave him some hitting advice and some worldly advice. Now I look in the paper, and I see how well he's doing in the Show and I get some real satisfaction. All I really did was try to keep him focused on ball and away from the day-to-day distractions that ruin concentration. The rest he did for himself.

The Writer: Do you ever wish you had done things differently?

The Ballplayer: No. Never. If I did it all over again, I would do it the same way. Don't know any different. Of course, if I did it all over again today, I don't think the media would make the same deal of it. I came along at a time when the country was in turmoil over race relations. I was an easy symbol and an easy target. The things I was saying then — a lot of those things — are hardly big news today.

The Writer: Sometimes I hear people say, "Dick Allen could have been another Hank Aaron. He could have had 800 career home runs. He could have batted .400. If only he had played by the rules." Any truth to it?

The Ballplayer: Somebody once said to my brother Hank, "If Dick had gone along, instead of bucking the system, he could have had 700 home runs and a .400 lifetime batting average." And Hank answered, "If Dick had gone along, he might have had 100 home runs and batted .220." I go along with that. You have to look at what is — not what could have been. I hit .300 seven times. I finished my career with 351 home runs. I was a starter on the All-Star team six times. I was a Rookie of the Year. I was an MVP. Dig?

The Writer: You still get a lot of votes for the Hall of Fame — fourteen the last time around. Is the Hall something you ever think about?

The Ballplayer: Who elects guys to the Hall of Fame? Sportswriters. You think they're going to get behind Dick

Allen? I don't care about the Hall of Fame. I do care about getting to heaven. Given the choice, I'll take heaven every time.

The Writer: How would you like to be remembered?

The Ballplayer: Everywhere I go, to this day, people come up to me and tell me stories about home runs they saw me hit. In Chicago, they remember the one I hit in the center-field bleachers in Comiskey. In Philly, they remember the shots that cleared the Coke and Cadillac signs on the roof. All that is flattering. But I want to be remembered as the complete ballplayer. As a guy who could steal a base, move a runner over, execute the squeeze. I also want to be remembered as a guy who played the game hard — very hard.

The Writer: Do you think you'll ever get back into baseball?

The Ballplayer: That's up to baseball. Baseball quit on me, I didn't quit on baseball.

The Writer: What kind of job would you like in baseball?

The Ballplayer: Not sure I would at all, but if I were to get back in, I'd like to work with young black ballplayers. I'd like to work with them while they're young before they've had a taste of fame. Tell them about my experiences and get them prepared for what life is like in the bigs. I'd like to talk to them about money and about the ladies that are going to come after them and about the agents that will want to sign them and about the owners who will want to use them and then discard them. Then, once I was sure they had their heads on straight about all that, I'd like to teach them the fundamentals — the lost art of baseball.

Epilogue

I love Dick Allen. How's that for straight down the middle? In the sixties and seventies, I loved Dick Allen as a ballplayer.

Now I love him as a friend.

I learned a lot about life from Dick Allen over the two years I spent with him.

I learned the art of being gentle. As an example, there was the time we had just finished a late-night dinner in a restaurant in Wampum, Pennsylvania, when I noticed Dick gathering up the uneaten rolls on the table and stuffing them in his pocket. When we got out to the parking lot afterward, Dick took out the rolls, carefully broke them into little pieces, and lined them up along a wall. "Breakfast for the birds," he said matter-of-factly.

On subsequent occasions, I saw Dick repeat the process, but never when anyone would notice. Now after a big meal out, I too find myself thinking about birds. My mother used to throw bread out for the birds every morning of her life. I had forgotten. In his fifteen years in baseball, Dick Allen had a lot of images and was called a lot of things. St. Francis of Assisi was never one of them.

I also learned some things about confidence. One of Dick's greatest loves (after baseball and horses) is boxing. In his day he was one of baseball's legendary shadowboxers. He would often shadowbox in the runways between the clubhouse and the dugout during games, most often just before coming to the plate; it was one of his favorite ways of getting it up to go *mano a mano* against the high hard one.

Dick had a series of shadowboxing partners in baseball, but in the mid-seventies his favorite combatant was Harold Watkins, a dugout security guard at Veterans Stadium. When I met Watkins in the process of doing this book, he regaled me with stories about Dick's shadowboxing prowess. "He can do Ali, Sugar Ray, Frazier, mimic them perfectly," Watkins told me. "He also has his own style, the Dick Allen shuffle. Fastest hands I've ever seen." Then Watkins confided something else. "I lost thirty pounds dancing away from Allen," he said proudly.

My first shadowbox session with Dick came in the parking lot of a Chicago hotel. The notion didn't come naturally to me. I was scrawny as a kid, and my favorite defense was to make friends with the guys who weren't. Dick began my lesson by teaching me to trust him. He placed my hands in front of my face and began, slowly at first, to throw some light jabs into my palms. When I didn't flinch, he escalated. His punches got harder and quicker and were delivered from all directions.

Once trust was established, it was my turn to swing at Dick. (Again, a concept I didn't relish.) At Dick's insistence I began to throw some halfhearted punches in his general direction, which he turned away effortlessly. But he soon demanded that I take the exercise more seriously, imploring me to throw my Sunday best. When I did, he caught each one cleanly in his palm with just the slightest flick of his wrist. He was clearly pleased at my effort and, with his encouragement, I was soon bobbing and weaving, firing lefts and rights in Dick's direction with near authority, and, more astonishingly — given my lack of predisposition to the sport — I began to deflect his return fire. When the lesson ended, we were both soaking wet.

In the two years since that first lesson, we've shadow-boxed together a number of times, and now I come out dancing. I've got a glide in my stride. As for Harold Watkins, he's maintained his new physique in the years following Dick's retirement — today, he proudly displays before and after photos in the rec room of his house. He always credits Dick with his streamlined body and what it's done for him. In my case, shadowboxing with Dick taught me a lot about trust and not a little bit about handling myself. Though I still think my tendency would be to head south if a fight ever broke out in my direction, I now know what I would do if somebody began giving me a hard time.

Call Dick Allen.

As unlikely as it may seem, I learned a lot about journalism, too — particularly sports journalism — from my many months of being with Dick Allen.

When I was growing up, my heroes were ballplayers and sportswriters, and not necessarily in that order. When my dad would take me to ballgames at Philadelphia's old Connie Mack Stadium, I would usually have my binoculars trained on the playing field. But after a big play or an important hit, I would spin around to take a quick look up to the press box. I felt as much excitement watching the writers furiously bang at their typewriters as I did watching the ball career off the Ballantine scoreboard. Back then, I viewed baseball not so much as the National Pastime as the Romantic Pastime, and the writers were as much a part of that romance as the guys on the field.

But after spending time with Dick, I began to reassess the sportswriting profession I had once romanticized. In going over clips of his career, I found the kind of vitriolic prose usually reserved for perpetrators of the worst kind of violent crime. One Philadelphia writer called Dick "a con man with muscles," another labeled him "a schizophrenic," and yet another felt free to satirize his diet, calling it "equally divided between imported and domestic." The attacks were venal and belittling and, with rare exception, bereft of an understanding of the inherent complexities in Dick's personality.

What's more, the assessments of his personality didn't jibe with the relationship I was beginning to forge with Dick myself. Had Dick changed that much since leaving baseball? Or were the sportswriters of the day simply unable or unwilling to deal with one of the game's most sensitive and complex personalities?

When I went over these clips with Dick and asked him about their tone and accuracy, he always shot back the same answer — "Why don't you ask the ballplayers?"

And so, over two summer seasons of working on this book, I did.

When I asked Bob Gibson, the Hall of Fame pitcher and former Allen teammate about Dick's treatment by the sporting press, I got back a parable. He told me of the time he himself had been ambushed by sportswriters in St. Louis for a comment about the installation of that city's Gateway Arch.

At the time, Gibson explained, there had been a lot of static from the black community in St. Louis surrounding the arch project, and some people thought the money could have been better spent on aiding the city's poor.

Gibson recalls: "So I'm getting out of my car to go into the ballpark. It's a night when I'm the starting pitcher. All of a sudden a bunch of writers run up and start grilling me on what I think of the arch. I said, 'Fuck the arch.' What I meant was, I got a job to do, and you're getting in my fuckin' way. But instead, they write it up like I don't care about the arch, I don't care about the black community." And about Dick Allen? "That's what I'm saying. Dick was the same way I was. You don't get in our way when we got ball to play. We've got baseball on our mind. Why didn't the writers ever figure that out? Why didn't the headlines ever say, GIBSON AND ALLEN CARE TOO MUCH ABOUT BALL TO MAKE SMALL TALK?"

When I asked Willie Stargell, another Hall of Famer, how he perceived Dick's treatment by the media, he gave me a historical perspective. Said Stargell: "Dick Allen played the game in the most conservative era in baseball history. It was a time of change and protest in the country, and baseball reacted against all that. They saw it as a threat to the game. The sportswriters were reactionary too. They didn't like seeing a man of such extraordinary skills doing it his way. It made them nervous. Dick Allen was ahead of his time. His views and ways of doing things would go unnoticed today. If I had been the manager of the Phillies back when he was playing, I would have found a way to make Dick comfortable. I would have told him to blow off the writers. It was always my observation that when Dick Allen was comfortable, balls left the park."

One of Dick's baseball buddies, Orlando Cepeda, was quick to give me his analysis: "What they did to Richie was wrong, man. Gave him a label that wasn't him. Richie played with fire in his eyes, always. Never read that in no newspaper. When I was with the Giants, and all those fans would start booing him when he came to the plate, I would yell for him to hit the ball out of the park. I would yell to him in Spanish so nobody knew. But Richie understands Spanish, so I know he knew."

Mike Schmidt, who played with Dick in the mid-seventies: "Guys used to write that Dick would divide the clubhouse along racial lines. Total bullshit. You walk into any major league clubhouse today and you'll see the black guys at one end listening to black music and the white guys at the other end listening to country music. It was that way in Dick Allen's era, and it's that way today. In all my years I've never seen it different. Dick never divided any clubhouse. He just got guys thinking."

Armed with such testimonies, I spoke with Larry Merchant, today a boxing analyst for HBO. In the sixties and seventies, Merchant had covered Dick as both an editor and a writer, first for the *Philadelphia Daily News* and later for the *New York Post*. I asked Merchant why Dick was so brutalized by the scribes of his day. "In terms of hot copy," Merchant explained, "Richie Allen was right up there with the epic personalities of the sixties. Everything was so titanic about Allen — from his home runs into the light towers to his fights with management. He was a walking headline. He was the guy everybody wanted to write about. Problem was, he didn't understand the relationship between the press and a superstar. He didn't take any responsibility for his image."

But didn't the writers have some responsibility to themselves and their readers to understand and interpret Dick's complex personality, superstar or no?

"Maybe. But understand, Allen was a good story — and that's what journalism is all about. Getting the story. Look, when a guy gets in a fight with a teammate, then doesn't show up at the ballpark a few times and blames it on traffic, then pushes his hand through a headlight, things escalate to the point where everybody just thinks he's a fuck-up, and that's what we wrote."

So there it is. The facts of sportswriting life. Forget the romantic calling. With rare exceptions, sportswriting is a business of deadlines and headlines. Forget the subtleties. Get the quotes, stir the controversy, satisfy the masses. If an athlete doesn't fit the cookie cutter, he's fucked. If you're a Dick Allen, you're double-fucked.

Friendship can't be one-sided, and my friendship with Dick works both ways. Our relationship could have gone differently. Other writers I know who have collaborated on books with ballplayers have invariably ended up with sour feelings toward their subjects. The relationship is inherently problematic: on the surface, the writer appears to do all the work while the subject does little more than blow hot air into a tape recorder.

But from the start, Dick and I shared equal responsibility for this project. There were no easy sit-down tape-recorder sessions. Dick trusted me with the most intimate details of his life, in his time, and in turn I guarded them closely. When I asked, I was given total access. When I felt it necessary to spend time with Barbara Moore, Dick's ex-wife, it was Dick himself who arranged it — even though he knew I would hear things that would not portray him in the best light.

I spent an evening together with Dick and Barbara, watched them laugh and reminisce, struggle and argue. They had shared a lot together, and it showed. I empathized with Barbara, a tough-minded woman who had single-handedly put the three Allen offspring through college. She is an eloquent woman. And I felt for Dick, as he explained his life, his love for his mother, his early baseball days, and how difficult it is to handle marriage with baseball as a first love. I spent time with the Allen children, good-looking, articulate, and well mannered all three, and realized that despite bearing witness to tragedies and stormy passions, they were the products of compassionate parents.

Dick also cared about me, not as a biographer, but as a person. He got to know my wife and my background and asked me about projects unrelated to our work. When it was time to talk, we got serious. When it was time for fun, we knew how. When we began working together, I had just come off a difficult time in my life. I had lost my mother and a young brother to cancer. I was struggling with depression. Instinctively, Dick knew what I was going through, the way people who have weathered difficult emotional times always do. When we'd go out together, I would sometimes tell him a bit of what I was feeling, and Dick would listen. When I finished we would spend a few moments together in respectful silence. And then we'd party. It was good medicine.

Summer '88: It is the twilight of Mike Schmidt's baseball career in Philadelphia. He is sitting in the Phillies dugout. His shoulder hurts. His legs are tired. He has a faraway look in his eyes. He knows his time in the game is short.

I interrupt his solitary reverie to ask him about Dick Allen, and when I do, he jumps to his feet, grabs a bat, and assumes the batting stance. He lowers his left shoulder and tugs at his shirt sleeves. He is snorting angrily through his nose. He is doing Dick Allen.

"This is the way he used to do it," says Mike Schmidt, smiling in a way you never see Mike Schmidt smile. "When I was playing Legion ball in Ohio, I always pretended I was Dick Allen. He was my idol."

Schmidt takes a healthy cut at the summer air. Then another. And another. He is playing imaginary baseball. And all the while, he is still smiling.

Dick Allen

BR TR 5'11" 187 lb.

ALLEN, RICHARD ANTHONY

Born March 8, 1942, Wampum, Pennsylvania
Brother of Hank Allen, former utilityman
with Washington Senators, Milwaukee
Brewers, and Chicago White Sox, and Ron
Allen, former first baseman with Philadelphia
Phillies and St. Louis Cardinals.

YR	TEAM	G	AB	H	2B	3B	HR	HR %	R	RBI	BB	SO	SB	BA	SA	Pinch Hit AB	Pinch Hit H	G by POS
1963	PHI N	10	24	7	2	1	0	0.0	6	2	0	5	0	.292	.458	2	0	OF-7, 3B-1
1964		162	632	201	38	13	29	4.6	125	91	67	138	3	.318	.557	0	0	3B-162
1965		161	619	187	31	14	20	3.2	93	85	74	150	15	.302	.494	1	0	3B-160, SS-2
1966		141	524	166	25	10	40	7.6	112	110	68	136	10	.317	.632	4	1	3B-91, OF-47
1967		122	463	142	31	10	23	5.0	89	77	75	117	20	.307	.566	1	0	3B-121, SS-1, 2B-1
1968		152	521	137	17	9	33	6.3	87	90	74	161	7	.263	.520	8	0	OF-139, 3B-10
1969		118	438	126	23	3	32	7.3	79	89	64	144	9	.288	.573	1	1	1B-117
1970	STL N	122	459	128	17	5	34	7.4	88	101	71	118	5	.279	.560	3	1	1B-79, 3B-38, OF-3
1971	LA N	155	549	162	24	1	23	4.2	82	90	93	113	8	.295	.468	3	0	3B-67, OF-60, 1B-28
1972	CHI A	148	506	156	28	5	37	7.3	90	113	99	126	19	.308	.603	7	1	1B-143, 3B-2
1973		72	250	79	20	3	16	6.4	39	41	33	51	7	.316	.612	3	0	1B-67, 2B-2, DH
1974		128	462	139	23	1	32	6.9	84	88	57	89	7	.301	.563	4	0	1B-125, 2B-1, DH
1975	PHI N	119	416	97	21	3	12	2.9	54	62	58	109	11	.233	.385	5	0	1B-113
1976		85	298	80	16	1	15	5.0	52	49	37	63	11	.268	.480	2	1	1B-85
1977	OAK A	54	171	41	4	0	5	2.9	19	31	24	36	1	.240	.351	2	0	1B-50, DH

YR TEAM	G	AB	H	2B	3B	HR	HR %	R	RBI	BB	SO	SB	BA	SA	Pinch Hit AB	H	G by POS
15 yrs.	1749	6332	1848	320	79	351	5.5	1099	1119	894	1556 8th	133	.292	.534	46	5	1B-807, 3B-652, OF-256, 2B-4, SS-3

LEAGUE CHAMPIONSHIP SERIES

YR TEAM	G	AB	H	2B	3B	HR	HR %	R	RBI	BB	SO	SB	BA	SA	Pinch Hit AB	H	G by POS
1976 PHI N	3	9	2	0	0	0	0.0	1	0	3	2	0	.222	.222	0	0	1B-3

ALL-STAR GAMES

YR	LEAGUE	AB	H	2B	3B	HR	RBI	BA	POS
1965	National	3	1	0	0	0	0	.333	3B
1966	National	1	0	0	0	0	0	.000	PH
1967	National	4	1	0	0	1	1	.250	3B
1970	National	3	0	0	0	0	0	.000	1B
1972	American	3	0	0	0	0	0	.000	1B
1974	American	2	1	0	0	0	1	.500	1B
6 yrs.		16	3	0	0	1	2	.188	

Named to American League All-Star Team for 1973; replaced due to an injury.